Echoes Of Atlantis, Legacy of the Gods

12,000 YEARS ONE EXTRAORDINARY TALE

RICHARD ECKLEY

Copyright © 2025 by Richard Eckley

All rights reserved.

No portion of this book may be reproduced in any form without written permission from the publisher or author, except as permitted by U.S. copyright law.

ISBN 978-1-9993147-9-8

Contents

Dedication		VI
1.	Echoes of Atlantis, Legacy of the Gods	1
2.	The Discovery at Gobekli Tepe	3
3.	Elena at Gobekli Tepe	9
4.	The Final Call From Hawara	10
5.	Elena With Her Father at Saqsayaman	17
6.	Ancient World Power	18
7.	Megalithic Structures Around The World	23
8.	Whispers Across Millennia	24
9.	Thothamak at Gobekli Tepe	29
10.	Thothamak's Sacred Stars	30
11.	Gobekli Tepe Aligning With The Stars	36
12.	The Golden Age of Giants	37
13.	Harbour at Atlantis	45

14.	Titans of Land and Legacy	46
15.	Atlanteans With The Megafauna of 12,000 Years Ago	53
16.	The Edge of Empire	54
17.	Ozymandias With The Atlantean Army	62
18.	Tide of War	63
19.	Atlantean Megaship With Orichalcum Heat Weapon	76
20.	Shadows of Youth	77
21.	Thothamak and Ozymandias escaping the shortfaced bear	90
22.	The Final Warning	91
23.	Asteroid Spotted by Astronomers	102
24.	When Atlantis Fell	103
25.	Asteroid Impacting The Ice Sheet	114
26.	Sanctuary in Shadow	115
27.	Tsunami Consuming Atlantis	133
28.	When Giants Fell	134
29.	Thothamak Viewing The Devastation After The Tsunami	147
30.	Sea of Memories	148
31.	Holding A Vigil In The Muddy Sea	158
32.	Legacy in Stone	159
33.	The Lybrinth at Hawara	174
34.	The Bearers of Light	175
35.	Thothamak Saying Goodbye To The Seven Sages	185

36.	The Seven Personal Laws	186
37.	The Seven Atlantean Laws Tablet	195
38.	The Bridge Between	196
39.	Elena Feeling Thothamak And Her Fathers Spirits Guiding Her	204
40.	The Legacy Discovered	205
41.	The Seven Atlantean Laws Of Advancement Continued	224
42.	Elena Finding Her Father's Journals	248
43.	Epilogue The Next Wave	249
44.	A New Threat Enters Our Cosmos	255
	About The Author	256
	Also by	258
	Atlantis A New Theory	266
	Coffee Reads Series	267
	Eckley Global Community School	268

Thank you for reading this book,
I hope you enjoy reading it as much as I did researching it

DEDICATION

To the seekers of lost histories,
who dare to look beyond accepted truths
and peer into the mists of time.

To those who understand that every grain of sand
holds a story, every ancient stone whispers secrets,
and legends often carry seeds of forgotten facts.

To the dreamers and scholars alike
who know that yesterday's myths
may be tomorrow's discoveries.

And to all those who believe that beneath
our modern world lie countless untold tales,
waiting to be unearthed by curious minds

and brave hearts.
May you find in these pages echoes of truths
yet to be discovered.

Echoes of Atlantis, Legacy of the Gods

Introduction

In the heart of modern-day Turkey, beneath the sun-baked earth of Göbekli Tepe, a farmer's spade struck not just ancient stones, but the very foundations of a forgotten world. As the dust of millennia settled, revealing intricate carvings and towering pillars, a gateway to the past cracked open, beckoning all who dared to peer through its impenetrable veil.

But Göbekli Tepe was more than a mere archaeological site; it was a whisper from ages long gone, a call to those who sought to unravel the mysteries of a bygone era. Little did the excavators know that their discoveries would bridge the chasm between myth and reality, connecting the present to a time when gods walked the earth and empires rose and fell like waves upon the shore.

As the sun dipped below the horizon, casting long shadows over the ancient stones, a story began to unfold—one that stretched back twelve thousand years to a land of legend and lore, where Poseidon, God of the seas, and his mortal love, Cleito, forged a realm that would echo through the annals of time. Atlantis, a kingdom of wonders and ambitions, stood as a beacon of power and prosperity, until the tides of fate shifted, and the winds of war swept across its shores.

Join us on this journey, where destiny is shared by gods and mortals alike, where the clash of civilizations reverberates through the ages, and where a celestial omen heralds a cataclysmic event that will shape the course of history.

Step through the portal of Göbekli Tepe and witness the echoes of Atlantis resounding across the sands of time, beckoning you to uncover the secrets buried beneath the rubble of ancient ruins. The adventure awaits, dear reader, as we embark on a quest to unveil the enigmatic past and illuminate the path to a future yet unwritten.

The Discovery at Gobekli Tepe

In the honeyed light of dawn, an old farmers weathered hands gripped the wooden plough as his oxen trudged forward, their breath misting in the cool morning air. The iron blade sliced through dark earth that had lain undisturbed for millennia, then an impact sent a shudder through the plough's handles and vibrating up his hands – metal striking something far more unyielding than soil. The old man's calloused fingers traced the edge of what appeared to be worked stone, its surface bearing the deliberate marks of human tools. As he scraped away centuries of accumulated earth, his heart quickened at the sight of geometric patterns emerging from the soil, their precision suggesting this was no natural formation.

He reached for his spade and started to dig around it, with each careful stroke, more of the structure revealed itself: Rising from the earth like the crown of a buried giant, the structure defied modern understanding. Its scale and sophistication challenged everything archaeologists thought they knew about prehistoric human capabilities. Here, in this quiet corner of Turkey, the dawn light illuminated not just stone and soil, but a mystery that would rewrite the story of human civilization.

As news of the discovery spread like wildfire through the countryside, a team of archaeologists descended upon the site, with the promise of unlocking a puzzle older than memory itself. The farmer, his weathered face etched with wonder, stood at the edge of the excavation pit, watching as the past unfurled before his very eyes.

The top of the stone pillar gleamed in the sunlight, adorned with intricate carvings of long-forgotten symbols and figures. Each chiselled line spoke of a civilization lost to time, a people who had toiled and dreamed beneath the same sun that now cast its benevolent gaze upon the scene.

As the archaeologists meticulously cleared away the layers of dirt and debris, the true extent of the discovery began to emerge. Circular structures, massive stone pillars, and intricate reliefs adorned with anthropomorphic details painted a picture of a society steeped in ritual and reverence for the divine.

Among the team of excavators, a young archaeologist named Elena stood transfixed before the ancient stones, her fingers tracing the weathered carvings with a mixture of trepidation and fascination. In that moment, she felt a connection to the past, a tug of destiny that beckoned her to unravel the mysteries that lay buried beneath the earth.

As the excavation delved deeper into the earth, the ancient stones whispered tales of a time long before memory, a time when gods walked among mortals and legends were born. Each carving, each pillar, held a piece of the puzzle, waiting to be pieced together by those who dared to venture into the heart of the past.

Elena, her eyes alight with curiosity and determination, led the team of archaeologists with a steady hand and a heart hungry for knowledge. Her nights were spent pouring over ancient texts and maps, seeking clues to unlock the secrets of Göbekli Tepe and the civilization it guarded within its silent stones.

At twenty-seven years old, she possessed a rare blend of intellect and adventurous spirit that set her apart in the world of archaeology. Her jet-black hair cascaded down her back in loose waves, framing a face that bore the faint traces of the sun's kiss from her travels to far-flung lands.

Her hazel eyes, flecked with hints of gold, sparkled with a thirst for knowledge and a passion for unravelling the mysteries of the past. Tall and slender, with a grace that belied her determination, Elena moved through the ruins with a sense of purpose, her every step a testament to her unwavering commitment to uncovering the secrets that lay hidden within the stones and sands.

Elena's love for archaeology was not merely a profession but a calling that had been woven into the fabric of her being from a young age. Growing up she had accompanied her father, a renowned archaeologist, on his expeditions to ancient sites around the world. It was during these travels that she fell in love with the stories of the past, the thrill of discovery, and the sense of connection to civilizations long gone.

Her father's passion for uncovering the truths buried beneath layers of time had ignited a spark within Elena, shaping her into the intrepid explorer and scholar she had become. Together, they had traversed the sun-baked deserts of Egypt, the misty mountains of Peru, the rugged landscapes of Bolivia, the ancient ruins of Turkey, and many more prehistoric sites around the world, forging a bond that transcended mere father and daughter to become fellow seekers of knowledge and guardians of history.

Elena's father, a seasoned archaeologist with a twinkle in his eye and a wealth of knowledge at his fingertips, had regaled her with tales of ancient legends that spoke of grand cities hidden deep within the Amazon rainforest, colossal complexes buried beneath the shifting sands of the Sahara Desert, and mythical civilizations now lost beneath the waves of the oceans.

As a young girl, Elena had listened with rapt attention as her father painted vivid pictures of these fabled cities, describing towering pyramids rising from the jungle canopy, sprawling metropolises carved into the rock of desert cliffs, and majestic palaces that gleamed like jewels beneath the azure waters of the seas.

The stories he shared kindled a fire of curiosity within her, igniting a thirst for adventure and discovery that would shape her future as an archaeologist and explorer. With each tale he told, Elena's imagination soared, envisioning herself standing amidst the ruins of ancient civilizations, unravelling the mysteries of lost worlds, and piecing together the fragments of history that had faded into myth and legend.

As a dedicated archaeologist and scholar of lost civilizations, he had devoted years of research to unravelling the mysteries surrounding mythical lands such as Lemuria, Mu, and the legendary Atlantis. His study of ancient texts, geological evidence, and historical accounts had led him down a path of discovery that had captivated his imagination and fuelled his quest for knowledge.

Lemuria, a fabled land said to have once existed in the Indian Ocean, was believed to be a lost continent that had vanished beneath the waves in a cataclysmic event of untold proportions. The tales of Lemuria spoke of a thriving civilization of advanced beings who possessed great wisdom and knowledge, but whose hubris had led to their downfall.

Mu, another enigmatic land shrouded in myth and legend, was said to have been located in the Pacific Ocean, with its own rich history and culture that rivalled even the most advanced civilizations of its time. The stories of Mu painted a picture of a paradise lost, a utopian society that had succumbed to the forces of nature and the whims of fate.

And then there was Atlantis, the most famous of all lost lands, whose tale had captured the hearts and minds of scholars, explorers, and dreamers for centuries. Believed to have been a mighty empire that once spanned the vast ocean between Europe and the Americas, Atlantis was said to have possessed technology and knowledge far beyond that of any known civilization of its time.

Elena's father had delved deep into the annals of history, piecing together fragments of ancient texts, deciphering cryptic symbols, and pouring over maps and artifacts in search of clues that would lead him to the elusive whereabouts of these lost lands and vanished continents. His quest had taken him to the farthest reaches of the earth, to places both real and imagined, as he sought to unravel the enigma that had eluded scholars and explorers for millennia.

As he shared his findings and theories with Elena, the young archaeologist-in-training listened with a mixture of awe and reverence, absorbing the knowledge and wisdom he imparted with a hunger for understanding that mirrored his own. Together, they poured over maps and charts, debated theories and hypotheses, and pieced together the puzzle of lost lands and vanished continents with a shared passion and determination that bound them together in their quest for truth.

As they stood on the precipice of discovery, with the echoes of ancient empires and lost civilizations reverberating in their ears, Elena and her father knew that the answers they sought lay just beyond the horizon, waiting to be unearthed and brought into the light of day. The mystery of Lemuria, Mu, and Atlantis beckoned to them, calling them to unlock the secrets of the past and reveal the truths that had been lost to time.

Elena at Gobekli Tepe

The Final Call From Hawara

Chapter 1

The shrill ring of the phone pierced the stillness of the night, jolting Elena from her reverie and sending a shiver of anticipation down her spine. She reached for the receiver, her fingers trembling with a mixture of excitement and trepidation, as she brought it to her ear and uttered a hesitant "Hello?"

On the other end of the line, her father's voice crackled with static, his words rushing forth like a torrent of revelation and wonder. "Elena, my dear, you won't believe what I've uncovered," he exclaimed, his tone filled with excitement. "I've found it, the Labyrinth at Hawara."

Elena's heart skipped a beat, her breath catching in her throat at the magnitude of her father's words. The Labyrinth near lake Moeris, the very same ones that the famed historian Herodotus had written about in his chronicles of the ancient world,

Her father's voice, tinged with a sense of urgency urged her to join him in Egypt, to witness firsthand the unveiling of the truths that had eluded scholars and explorers for centuries.

"Elena, you must come," he implored, "Together, we will unlock the secrets of Atlantis and uncover the mysteries of a lost world. I've seen the scrolls in there, tablets and ancient hieroglyphs, you're so much better at reading them now my eyes are fading. I'm heading there now, I have uncovered a secret door, by the time I clear it you will be here, and we can open it together"

But as Elena listened to her father's impassioned plea, a sense of foreboding crept into her heart, a whisper of doubt that niggled at the edges of her mind. The heat of the Egyptian sun, the oppressive weight of the desert sands, the relentless march of time itself – all these factors converged in her thoughts, painting a picture of danger and uncertainty that made her stomach churn with unease.

As the crackling voice of her father echoed through the phone line, Elena's heart quickened, this revelation that reached back into the mists of antiquity and beckoned her to follow in his footsteps on a journey of mystery and wonder could be a step too far for her father.

Her father's voice carried a sense of urgency that was palpable even through the static of the connection. "I have found the Labyrinth", he said "It surpasses even the magnificence of the Egyptian pyramids, I managed to crawl through a crack in the door."

The mention of the Labyrinth, a fabled construction shrouded in myth and legend, sent a thrill of anticipation coursing through Elena's veins. The intricate details her father shared about the structure – its twelve roofed courts, its double sets of chambers numbering three thousand in total, its underground passages and many corridors – conjured up images of a place of unparalleled complexity and grandeur, a testament to the ingenuity and skill of the ancient builders who had brought it into being.

"We learned through conversation about its underground chambers," her father continued, his voice filled with excitement. "The Egyptian caretakers guard what's left of it zealously, claiming they are the burial vaults of the kings who first constructed the Labyrinth, as well as the resting place of sacred crocodiles. The upper chambers, those we were able to explore, are nothing short of miraculous in their craftsmanship and design, a sight to behold for any who dare to venture within."

Elena listened intently, her mind racing with visions of the Labyrinth's grandeur and complexity, its walls adorned with cut figures and its courts lined with pillars of white stone. The mention of a pyramid standing near the labyrinth's end, its towering height and intricate carvings hinting at untold secrets and mysteries waiting to be uncovered, sent a shiver of excitement down her spine.

Her father's words painted a picture of a place where history and myth intertwined, where the echoes of the past whispered secrets long forgotten and truths waiting to be brought to light. The Labyrinth, with its enigmatic corridors and hidden chambers, beckoned to Elena with a siren's call, drawing her into a web of intrigue and discovery that would test her courage and her resolve like never before.

She begged her father to wait for her, to allow her the chance to join him and help in the mammoth task of clearing the door and share in the discovery that lay just beyond it. To put off the excavation for just a week, to allow her to finish off her work in Gobekli Tepi and join him for the rest of the archaeology season in Egypt. But he brushed aside her concerns, his voice filled with a fervour that brooked no opposition, his determination unyielding in the face of her pleas.

"No" he said, "Catch the next flight, this is more important, there are others nearby who will steal our find you must come now!"

"I can't" said Elena "Just give me a few days"

"There isn't time" he said, "leave now this is far more important!"

"I can't"

And then, in a moment that would haunt her for the rest of her days, Elena heard the telltale gasp, the sharp intake of breath that signalled the onset of a heart attack. Her father's words faltered, his voice fading into a whispered plea for forgiveness and understanding, as the line went silent, and the connection was lost.

Tears welled in Elena's eyes as she stood there, the phone slipping from her fingers and clattering to the floor, the weight of her father's revelation and his untimely demise crashing down upon her like a wave of sorrow and regret. The underground passages near the pyramid, the scripts hidden in the heart of the lake – all of it now lay shrouded in darkness, a mystery unsolved and a legacy left unfulfilled.

Her father's untimely death hit Elena like a thunderbolt, shattering the world she had known and plunging her into a maelstrom of grief and disbelief. The loss of her mentor, her guide, and her dearest friend left a void in her heart that seemed impossible to fill, a wound that throbbed with the ache of a thousand unspoken words and unfinished conversations.

Her father's final revelation, hung in the air like a spectre, haunting her with its tantalizing promise of knowledge and discovery. The ancient manuscript he had uncovered in Egypt, a treasure trove of secrets and revelations that had eluded scholars for centuries, now lay dormant, waiting to be brought to light by hands as skilled and as passionate as his own.

The phone call that had changed everything echoed in Elena's ears, the sound of her father's voice filled with excitement and urgency as he shared his discovery with her. She had pleaded with him to wait for her, to allow her to join him in Egypt and witness the unveiling of the truth together, but he had brushed aside her concerns, his passion and determination driving him forward despite the warnings of his doctors and the protests of his loved ones.

In his eighties, still wielding a trowel and a brush with the skill and finesse of a master craftsman, her father had defied the ravages of time and the constraints of age, his spirit unbroken and his thirst for knowledge undimmed by the passage of years. But the time bomb that had been ticking in his chest, a silent killer lurking in the shadows, had finally claimed him, snuffing out the flame of his life and leaving behind a legacy of unfinished dreams and unfulfilled promises.

As Elena stood amidst the relics of the past, surrounded by the echoes of ancient empires and lost civilizations, she felt a sense of duty and destiny descending upon her shoulders like a mantle of responsibility. The key to unlocking the secrets of a forgotten world, now lay in her hands, a torch passed from father to daughter, a legacy of knowledge and wisdom that beckoned her to carry on his work and fulfil his final wish.

With a resolve as steely as the blade of a sword and a heart as resolute as the stones of the pyramids, Elena vowed to honour her father's memory, to uncover the truth he had sacrificed everything to find, and to bring to light the secrets that had eluded him in life but would not escape her grasp. The journey ahead would be fraught with peril and uncertainty, but she would not falter, for she carried within her the spirit of a warrior and the soul of an explorer, driven by a passion for discovery and a thirst for knowledge that burned brighter than any flame.

Her father's words became a beacon of inspiration, Together, they had traversed the globe in search of truth and enlightenment, uncovering secrets that had lain hidden for centuries.

The Amazon rainforest, with its dense canopy and teeming biodiversity, held the promise of ancient wonders waiting to be unearthed. The Sahara Desert, vast and unforgiving, concealed secrets of civilizations lost to the sands of time. And the oceans, vast and mysterious, whispered tales of sunken cities and submerged kingdoms that lay waiting beneath the waves for those brave enough to seek them out.

As Elena stood at Göbekli Tepe, the tales her father had shared now echoed in her heart, filling her with a sense of purpose and destiny that drove her forward on a journey that would take her to the ends of the earth and beyond, in search of the truth that lay hidden beneath the veil of time. But she had to finish her work in Gobekli Tepe first, she would fly to Egypt the next day after closing her dig.

Elena With Her Father at Saqsayaman

Ancient World Power

Chapter 2

That evening, as the last rays of sunlight painted the sky in hues of crimson and gold, Elena made a discovery that would change the course of their excavation. A hidden chamber, within Gobekli Tepe concealed beneath layers of rubble and debris, revealed itself to her keen eye, beckoning her into its shadowed depths.

With trembling hands and a heart pounding with excitement, Elena stepped into the chamber, her lantern casting flickering shadows on the walls adorned with intricate carvings and inscriptions. Symbols of power, of gods and goddesses long forgotten, danced before her eyes, a patchwork of ancient wisdom and divine mysteries.

As she traced her fingers over the weathered stones, a sense of reverence washed over her, a feeling of standing on the threshold of something greater than herself. The chamber seemed to pulse with a life of its own, as if the very stones were alive with the echoes of a civilization that had been lost to time.

And in that moment, Elena knew that Göbekli Tepe held more than just archaeological significance—it held the key to unlocking a story that would change the course of history forever. Yet she felt she had to go to her father's side, to say goodbye to her mentor and the man who had installed all her beliefs and raised her into the independent woman she had become. Continuing His vision of ancient history that had been passed on to her.

However, even with the depth of sorrow she felt, she couldn't help but be drawn to the enigmatic connection shared by ancient observatories across the world, scattered like stardust across distant lands, they stood as silent sentinels to the heavens, their purpose shrouded in the mists of time.

From the towering stones of Stonehenge in England to the precise alignments of Machu Picchu in Peru, the intricate celestial calendar of Chichen Itza in Mexico to the enigmatic Nazca Lines, the ancient peoples of the world had erected monuments that gazed up at the stars with a sense of purpose and wonder.

The question that puzzled both modern scholars and ancient civilizations alike was how these structures, built with immense stones and intricate precision, had come to be. The alignment of these observatories with specific stars and celestial events suggested a level of astronomical knowledge and architectural skill that defied conventional understanding.

It seemed inconceivable that such monumental feats of engineering could have been accomplished independently by disparate civilizations across the globe. The precision with which these observatories were aligned to the stars spoke of a shared purpose, a common quest to unlock the mysteries of the cosmos and chart the movements of the heavens.

As Elena pieced together fragments of ancient myths and legends, she began to see a pattern emerge—a connection of celestial lore, architectural marvels, and a shared legacy of knowledge passed down through generations. The idea of a vast empire, a civilization that spanned continents and shared its wisdom with distant lands, took root in her mind like a seed waiting to bloom. How she wished she could share these thoughts with her father.

Could it be that an ancient empire, one that had long faded into the annals of history, once held sway over the world, guiding civilizations in the art of celestial observation and architectural mastery? The implications of such a revelation were staggering, hinting at a legacy of exploration and discovery that transcended the boundaries of time.

With each discovery made at Göbekli Tepe, Elena felt the threads of history drawing her closer to a truth that had lain hidden for millennia. The ancient observatories stood as silent witnesses to a bygone age, their stones whispering tales of a time when the world was united in its quest to unravel the mysteries of the cosmos.

Memories of her past expeditions with her father to ancient sites around the world flooded her mind like a torrential river of knowledge and wonder. She closed her eyes and let the echoes of Saksaywaman,

Baalbek, Cuzco, the Great Pyramid of Egypt, Tiwanaku, Gunung Padang and Puma Punku wash over her, each site a testament to the ingenuity and skill of ancient civilizations.

In Cuzco at Saksaywaman, high in the Andes mountains, she had marvelled as her father showed her the precision with which the massive stones were fitted together, so tight that not even a blade could slip between them. forming walls that defied the passage of time. The size of the stones, some weighing hundreds of tons, and the intricate building techniques used to create the site hinted at a level of engineering prowess that surpassed modern understanding.

At Baalbek, in the heart of Lebanon, Elena had argued with her father theorising how the blocks could be cut and moved then raised into position, they had both stood in awe before the colossal stone blocks that made up the Temple of Jupiter. The sheer magnitude of the stones, some weighing over 1,000 tons, and the seamless precision with which they were aligned spoke of a civilization capable of feats that seemed impossible by contemporary standards. The similarity in building techniques to those found at other ancient sites around the world hinted at a shared knowledge and expertise passed down through generations.

The Great Pyramid of Egypt, standing as a sentinel on the Giza plateau, had beckoned her father and Elena to unravel its mysteries. The massive limestone and granite blocks that formed its core, each weighing several tons, and the precise alignment of the pyramid's sides with the cardinal points of the compass hinted at a level of mathematical and astronomical understanding that boggled the mind.

In Tiwanaku, on the shores of Lake Titicaca in Bolivia, they had gazed upon the monolithic statues and finely crafted stonework of the ancient city, pondering the techniques used to create such intricate structures. The nearby megalithic stones of Puma Punku, with their precise cuts and interlocking shapes and engineered drilled holes, whispered of a civilization with a mastery of stone unlike any other.

Then Gunung Padang possibly the oldest ancient site so far discovered, made of thousands of tons of basalt blocks, layer upon layer each civilization building on the last, going back possibly to over 20,000 years.

As Elena connected the dots between these ancient sites, a pattern emerged—of shared knowledge, building techniques, and a reverence for the heavens. The similarities in stone size, construction methods, and astronomical alignments pointed to a common heritage, a civilization that spanned the globe and left its mark on the stones that bore witness to its greatness.

With each memory of her journeys to these ancient sites the realization dawned on her, like the first light of day, illuminating a path that led back to Göbekli Tepe and the enigmatic stones that held the key to unlocking the secrets of a bygone era—a time when a great empire united the world in its quest for knowledge and understanding. With a deep breath and a heart filled with determination, she raised her lantern high, ready to illuminate the shadows of the past and reveal the truth hidden within the ancient stones of Göbekli Tepe itself.

Megalithic Structures Around The World

Whispers Across Millennia

Chapter 3

Her father had uncovered tantalizing references to a cataclysmic event that had obliterated a once-great empire, plunging the world into an age of darkness and despair. The fragmented accounts he had meticulously pieced together spoke of a time when the heavens themselves seemed to mourn, their tears cascading upon a world that had lost its brilliance. The earth, too, had borne witness to the tragedy, trembling in anguish as it swallowed the remnants of a civilization that had once aspired to touch the stars.

He had staked his reputation—his life's work—on this theory, convinced that the truth lay buried far deeper than modern excavations dared to explore. The evidence, he argued, was there, waiting to be unearthed. With each meter of soil corresponding to nearly a millennium of history, the average archaeological dig rarely ventured beyond the Roman layer at a depth of two meters. Scholars and archaeologists, whether due to caution, scepticism, or fear of the unknown, had hesitated to dig further, stopping short of uncovering the secrets buried in the strata below.

But her father had been resolute, unwavering in his belief that the cataclysm had occurred at a depth of at least ten meters—some 32 feet beneath the surface of the earth. This was the layer where the ruins of the ancient world lay entombed, hidden from view and untouched by modern hands. He was certain that even more ancient sites, relics of civilizations predating known history, lay buried even deeper, beneath centuries of sediment and time's relentless accumulation.

Only in the future, he had often said, when humanity dared to dig deeper—both physically and intellectually—would we finally begin to piece together the truth of our past. Only then could we uncover the full scope of the ancestors' achievements and perhaps even learn from the mistakes that had led to their downfall. For now, the answers lay just out of reach, shrouded in history's veils.

The more she recalled her father's words, the more she became convinced that the key to understanding the mysteries of Göbekli Tepe and its global counterparts lay in the distant past, a time when an ancient empire flourished, and the world was a playground of wonder and discovery. The echoes of that lost era reverberated through the ages, calling out to those who dared to listen and learn.

In the stillness of the ancient chamber at Gobekli Tepe, bathed in the shadows of the night, Elena closed her eyes and let the memories of her father flood her mind, a bittersweet symphony of moments shared, and lessons learned echoing in the depths of her soul. As she stood amidst the towering pillars and intricate carvings of the long-forgotten temple, a sense of connection to the past enveloped her, drawing her into a trance-like state where time seemed to lose its grasp and the boundaries between then and now blurred into obscurity.

In that moment of profound stillness, a strange sensation overcame Elena, as if the very air around her shimmered with unseen energies and whispered secrets of ages long gone. She felt a presence, ancient and powerful, reaching out to her from the depths of history, at first a muffled voice seemed to greet her, welcoming her into the chamber as one of their own. The words spoken were unfamiliar yet resonant, a language lost to time but understood in the deepest recesses of her being.

As Elena delved deeper into the trance-like state that held her captive, she felt herself transported across the vast expanse of millennia, back to a time when Gobekli Tepe stood in all its glory, a beacon of civilization and knowledge in a world shrouded in mystery and wonder. The builders of this sacred site, the architects of its grandeur and majesty, surrounded her like phantoms from the past, their presence palpable and their voices clear in her mind.

She listened intently, her heart pounding with a mixture of fear and trepidation, as the ancient builders shared their wisdom and insights with her, revealing the secrets of their craft and the purpose behind the monumental structures they had erected with such precision and skill. They spoke of a time of great upheaval and change, of a world in flux and a people on the cusp of transformation, guided by visions and prophecies that spoke of a future yet to unfold.

In that timeless moment of communion with the spirits of the past, Elena felt a sense of belonging and purpose unlike any she had experienced before. The echoes of ancient voices reverberated through her being, filling her with a sense of admiration and reverence for the mysteries that lay hidden within the stones and symbols of Gobekli Tepe.

Twelve thousand years slipped away like grains of sand in an hourglass, and Elena found herself standing at the threshold of a new chapter in the saga of the lost civilization. The mists of time parted before her, revealing a landscape of ancient wonders and forgotten truths,

And then, as if summoned by her presence, a voice resonated through the air, a voice that bore the weight of authority and knowledge accumulated over centuries of craftsmanship and dedication. "Change the position on that stone," the head architect's directive pierced through the veil of time, his words carrying a sense of urgency and purpose. "It isn't lining up with Sirius, and the carvings need to be deeper into the stone. We must align our work with the celestial bodies above, for they hold the key to unlocking the secrets of the universe."

Her eyes fixed shut she visioned a figure of the head architect standing before her, his form illuminated by the flickering light of torches that cast dancing shadows across the ancient stones. Clad in garments of woven linen and adorned with symbols of his craft, he exuded an aura of wisdom and command that held her spellbound.

The head architect's words echoed in the chamber, a reminder of the meticulous precision and reverence for the cosmos that had guided the hands of the builders at Göbekli Tepe. Every carving, every alignment with the stars above, had been imbued with meaning and purpose, a testament to the spiritual beliefs and astronomical knowledge of those who had raised the massive stone pillars millennia ago.

As Elena stood in the depths of Göbekli Tepe, the head architect's voice still ringing in her ears, she felt a surge of determination well up within her. To be in the presence of such ancient wisdom, to witness the legacy of a civilization that had gazed upon the same stars and pondered the same mysteries of the universe.

Thothamak at Gobekli Tepe

Thothamak's Sacred Stars

Chapter 4

12,000 years earlier the head architect overseeing the construction of Göbekli Tepe, known for his unparalleled knowledge of astronomy and celestial alignments, bore the name Thothemak, a name that resonated with the echoes of ancient wisdom and divine inspiration. As he stood amidst the towering T-shaped pillars and intricate carvings of the site, Thothemak's gaze was fixed upon the heavens above, his mind attuned to the movements of the celestial bodies that held the key to unlocking the future course of humanity.

With a voice that carried the authority of a sage and the clarity of a seer, Thothemak instructed his craftsmen and artisans to ensure that Göbekli Tepe was built in its exact position to view the night sky, allowing them to track the movements of the seven planets that glided across the heavens. He emphasized the importance of aligning the structure with the stars above, guiding his followers to create a sacred space that mirrored the cosmic order and harmony of the universe itself.

As the night sky shimmered with the celestial bodies that held sway over the fate of mortals and immortals alike, Thothemak gathered his disciples beneath the shadow of Göbekli Tepe to impart upon them the sacred wisdom of the heavens. Pointing to the pillars that rose like sentinels against the backdrop of the starlit sky, he spoke of the importance of aligning the structure with the planets, or gods, whose movements dictated the ebb and flow of life on Earth.

"These pillars must be in perfect harmony with the gods," Thothemak began, his voice carrying the weight of centuries of astronomical knowledge and spiritual insight. "Each pillar represents a connection to the divine realm, a link between the earthly domain and the celestial spheres above. By aligning our sacred site with the paths of the planets, we honour the gods and ensure their benevolent influence upon our endeavours."

Pointing to the first pillar, Thothemak spoke of Selenê, the Greek goddess of the Moon, whose silvery light guided travellers through the darkness and inspired poets and dreamers alike. "Selenê watches over us from the night sky, her gentle gaze a reminder of the cycles of renewal and transformation that shape our lives," he explained, his eyes reflecting the ethereal glow of the moon above.

Moving on to the next pillar, Thothemak invoked the name of Hermes, the Greek god associated with Mercury, known for his swiftness and cunning. "Hermes, the messenger of the gods, embodies the swift and agile qualities of Mercury, guiding our thoughts and communications with divine inspiration," he intoned, his words resonating with the quicksilver energy of the planet that danced across the heavens.

Continuing his teachings, Thothemak spoke of Aphroditê, the Greek goddess of love and beauty, associated with Venus, whose radiant beauty and passionate nature inspired love and creativity among mortals. "Aphroditê embodies the essence of Venus, her allure and grace a reflection of the planet's enchanting presence in the night sky," he declared, his voice suffused with reverence for the goddess of love and beauty.

Turning his gaze to the radiant orb that illuminated the heavens by day, Thothemak spoke of Helios, the Greek god of the Sun, whose golden chariot traversed the sky, bringing light and warmth to the world below. "Helios, the sun god, shines upon us with his divine radiance, his chariot a symbol of power and vitality that sustains all life on Earth," he proclaimed, his words resonating with the brilliance and majesty of the solar deity.

With each planet and its corresponding deity, Thothemak illuminated the interconnectedness of the cosmos and the earthly realm, showing his disciples the intricate web of influences that shaped their lives and destinies. From the fiery presence of Ares, the Greek god of war associated with Mars, to the regal stature of Zeus, the king of the gods in Greek mythology and counterpart to Jupiter, each planet held sway over different aspects of human experience and spiritual evolution.

He then spoke of the connection between Kronos and Saturn, to the cyclical nature of time, power, and transformation. "Kronos, the Titan lord of the Golden Age, wielded the scythe of destiny and ruled over a realm of eternal abundance and harmony," Thothemak began, his voice carrying the weight of ancient knowledge and reverence for the mythic figure.

"Saturn, the planet named in honour of Kronos, holds sway over time, structure, and discipline in the celestial spheres," Thothemak continued, his words resonating with the slow and steady movements of the ringed planet in the night sky. "Just as Kronos imposed order and limitation upon the world, so too does Saturn govern the boundaries and constraints that shape our lives and destinies."

With a sweep of his hand, Thothemak pointed to the distant orb of Saturn, its rings shimmering like a crown of ethereal beauty encircling the planet. "In the movements of Saturn through the heavens, we see the passage of time, the cycles of growth and decay, and the inevitability of change," he explained, his eyes reflecting the solemn wisdom of the ages.

As his disciples pondered the connection between Kronos and Saturn, they began to see the parallels between myth and reality, between the ancient tales of gods and titans and the celestial bodies that governed the movements of the universe. Through the lens of Thothemak's teachings, they gained a deeper understanding of the interconnectedness of the cosmic forces that shaped their world and their place within it.

Under Thothemak's guidance, Göbekli Tepe rose from the earth like a beacon of light, a testament to the ingenuity and spiritual wisdom of its builders. The site became a sanctuary where the mysteries of the cosmos and the secrets of the earth converged, a place where the boundaries between the physical and spiritual worlds blurred, and where the timeless dance of the planets above was mirrored in the sacred dance of life below.

Thothemak stood tall and commanding, a figure of imposing presence amidst the stones of Göbekli Tepe. At over 9 feet in height, he towered over his disciples with a strength and grace that spoke of his lineage and training as a priest-architect. His athletic build, honed through years of dedication to his craft, bore the marks of a man who had inherited a sacred legacy passed down through generations of his ancestors.

Born into a line of priest-architects that stretched back over thousands of years, to the island of Atlantis, Thothemak was no ordinary man. His father, his grandfather, and all the male ancestors before him had walked the path of the gods, blending the arts of priesthood and architecture in service to the divine. Trained at the Temple of Poseidon in Atlantis, Thothemak had mastered the esoteric knowledge of the ancients, learning the secrets of stone masonry, metallurgy, mathematics, geometry and astronomy connecting the stars and the ways of the gods under the watchful eye of his master.

With each step he took among the newly forming stones of Göbekli Tepe, he felt the weight of his heritage pressing upon him, a mantle of responsibility and honour that he bore with pride. His connection to the past, to the legendary figure of Atlas who held up the heavens, gave him strength and purpose in his quest to uphold the traditions of his forefathers and guide his disciples along the path of enlightenment.

As the work on Göbekli Tepe neared completion, Thothemak stood beneath the night sky, his eyes raised to the stars twinkling in the velvet darkness above. In that moment of perfect alignment between heaven and earth, between past and present, he knew that the legacy of Göbekli Tepe would endure for millennia to come, a testament to the enduring quest of humanity to unlock the secrets of the universe and find our place within it.

Gobekli Tepe Aligning With The Stars

The Golden Age of Giants

Chapter 5

Thothamak's thoughts drifted back through the mists of time to his legendary ancestor, the great Atlas whose name was synonymous with strength, wisdom, and the boundless expanse of the heavens. Atlas, the Titan who had shouldered the weight of the world itself, was not just a figure of myth and legend to Thothemak—he was a revered forefather whose spirit lived on in the blood that flowed through his veins.

In the hallowed halls of Atlantis, the city of Thothemak's birth and the seat of his ancestral line, the stories of Atlas's voyages and celestial navigation had been passed down through the ages like precious gems of wisdom. Atlas, the master astronomer and navigator, had sailed the oceans by the guidance of the stars, charting his course by the constellations that adorned the night sky and the movements of the planets that held sway over the fate of mortals and immortals alike.

Through his mastery of astronomy, Atlas had ventured to the four corners of the world, mapping his voyages with meticulous precision and sharing his knowledge and skills with the peoples he encountered along the way. From the towering peaks of the Himalayas to the sun-drenched shores of the Mediterranean, Atlas had left his mark upon the world, not through conquest or domination, but through education, trade, and the exchange of knowledge and ideas.

Thothemak following in Atlas's footsteps, had dedicated his life to the twin arts of priesthood and architecture, blending the sacred and the practical in service to the divine. The buildings he had erected in cities across the whole world stood as testaments to his skill and vision, the megaliths cut with such precision and mastery using a combination of metallurgy and stone masonry slicing through granite like a knife through butter, aligned to the cardinal points, north, south, east and west, monuments to a civilization that valued wisdom, harmony, and the pursuit of knowledge above all else.

In the halls of Atlantis, Thothemak had been taught that true power lay not in the wielding of swords or the trappings of wealth, but in the cultivation of the mind and the spirit. Through education and enlightenment, through the sharing of knowledge and the fostering of understanding between peoples, Atlantis had risen to become a global power, its influence extending far beyond its shores to touch the lives of all who sought wisdom and truth in a world beset by strife and ignorance. They had harnessed the power of the sun, sound and magnetism That wouldn't be mastered again for over 12,000 years.

Atlantis, positioned halfway between Europe and the Americas on the Mid Atlantic Ridge, with its shimmering white marble buildings that rose like pillars of light from the crystal-clear waters, was a sight to behold. Its streets were lined with statues of gods and heroes, its temples adorned with intricate carvings and golden friezes that told the stories of a civilization steeped in wisdom and harmony.

Each successive generation of kings embellished the palace, surpassing their predecessors in magnificence and grandeur, until the buildings stood as a testament to their power and vision - a marvel to behold for its sheer size and breathtaking beauty.

From the sea, the Atlanteans bore a canal of immense proportions - three hundred feet in width, one hundred feet in depth, and stretching fifty stadia in length "a stadia being around 600ft". This monumental canal was a feat of engineering prowess, connecting the sea to the outermost zone of the city. It served as a vital passageway, transforming into a bustling harbour that welcomed the largest vessels with ease, enabling trade and prosperity to flourish within the city's walls.

Furthermore, the Atlanteans divided the zones of land that separated the zones of sea with bridges, creating pathways for ships to navigate effortlessly from one zone to another. These bridges were meticulously designed to allow a single trireme to pass through, ensuring seamless access throughout the city's intricate waterways.

To enhance navigation and accessibility, the Atlanteans covered over the channels with raised banks, providing a clear passage for ships while maintaining a stable foundation for travel. Beneath the surface, a hidden network of waterways thrived, allowing ships to glide through the city with grace and ease, a true testament to the advanced maritime technology of the Atlanteans.

The Atlanteans, masters of craftsmanship and artistry, adorned the entirety of their city's outermost zone with a sheen of brass, creating a gleaming circuit of walls that encased their magnificent civilization in a radiant embrace. This outer wall, a symbol of strength and protection, stood as a testament to the Atlanteans' dedication to safeguarding their homeland.

Moving inward, the next circuit of walls that enveloped the city was coated with tin, adding a lustrous touch to the architectural marvel that surrounded the Atlantean realm. The tin-coated walls reflected the sunlight like a beacon of prosperity and sophistication, drawing the gaze of all who beheld them.

At the heart of the city, within the citadel that gleamed with the red light of orichalcum, the Atlanteans crafted their most sacred and revered structures. The palaces within the citadel were a sight to behold, each a testament to the grandeur and opulence of Atlantean architecture.

In the centre of the citadel stood a holy temple dedicated to Cleito and Poseidon, a place of reverence and mystery that remained inaccessible to all but the chosen few. Surrounded by an enclosure of gold, this temple was the sacred birthplace of the royal family, where the people brought offerings of the earth's bounty from all ten portions of the land in a yearly ritual of gratitude and reverence.

Within Poseidon's temple, a marvel of engineering and devotion, the Atlanteans lavished their skill and resources. The temple stretched a stadium in length and half a stadium in width, its proportions harmonious and awe-inspiring. The exterior of the temple, save for the pinnacles, was adorned with silver, while the pinnacles themselves gleamed with the brilliance of gold.

Inside the temple, a realm of opulence unfolded - the roof crafted from ivory intricately detailed with gold, silver, and orichalcum, the walls, pillars, and floor coated with the shimmering essence of orichalcum. Statues of gold adorned the sacred space, their silent presence a tribute to the gods and a reflection of the Atlanteans' reverence for their divine heritage.

The island where the magnificent palace stood spanned a diameter of five stadia, a testament to the grandeur and scale of the Atlantean realm. Encircling this island, along with the surrounding zones and the bridge - a marvel of engineering that was one-sixth of a stadium in width - the Atlanteans erected sturdy stone walls on all sides. Towers and gates adorned the bridges where the sea flowed gracefully into the heart of the city, marking the entrance points with a touch of regal splendour.

The stones used in this monumental construction were carefully quarried from beneath the central island and the zones, both outer and inner. These stones came in three distinct hues - white, black, and red - each symbolizing a different aspect of the Atlantean civilization. As they extracted the stone, the Atlanteans simultaneously carved out double docks, ingeniously crafting roofs from the very bedrock of the island itself.

Located in the midst of the great Atlantic Ocean, named after Atlas, himself, Atlantis was a realm unto itself, a jewel set in the azure embrace of the sea. Its people were skilled navigators, seafarers, and traders their ships ploughing the waves with a grace and speed that left other nations in awe. The Atlanteans had harnessed the power of the elements, using wind, sun and water to propel their vessels across the vast expanses of the ocean with a precision and skill that seemed almost magical.

But Atlantis was not just a centre of technological innovation—it was also a bastion of philosophy and enlightenment. The Atlanteans were scholars and thinkers, poets and artists, whose minds soared to the heights of knowledge and wisdom. In the great libraries and academies of the city, they delved into the mysteries of the cosmos, pondered the nature of existence, and sought to unlock the secrets of the universe itself.

Under the guidance of Poseidon, Atlantis had become a beacon of light and learning in a world shrouded in darkness and ignorance. The gods themselves looked upon the city with favour, seeing in its people a reflection of their own divine essence. And so, Atlantis flourished, its influence spreading far and wide, its name whispered in wonder by all who heard of its creations and marvels.

And thus, Poseidon's creation, Atlantis, stood as a testament to the boundless power of the gods, the ingenuity of mortals, and the enduring legacy of a civilization that had reached the pinnacle of achievement in both technology and philosophy. The tales of the immense size of the Atlanteans, standing at towering heights of ten feet or more, were whispered like echoes from a distant past around the world were these just men or an ancient line of gods?

As Thothemak delved deeper into the ancient scrolls and manuscripts that chronicled the history of Atlantis in its great library, he uncovered accounts of how the colossal stature of the Atlanteans had led to awe and reverence among the local inhabitants of the lands they visited.

As the Atlantean ships sailed across the vast oceans, propelled by the skill and navigation of their towering crews, the sight of these giants descending upon foreign shores struck fear and wonder into the hearts of the indigenous peoples. To the eyes of the locals, the Atlanteans appeared as gods come to guide them in the creation of civilization, their massive forms casting shadows that seemed to stretch to the very heavens.

The local inhabitants, their minds filled with superstition, fell to their knees before the Atlanteans, bringing offerings of fruits, flowers, and precious jewels, and even sacrificing animals in rituals meant to appease these towering beings. The Atlanteans, with their advanced knowledge of agriculture, architecture, and astronomy, seemed to possess powers and abilities beyond mortal ken, their very presence transforming the landscape and shaping the destiny of those who dwelt in their shadow.

With each passing day, the legend of the Atlanteans grew, their reputation as divine beings spreading far and wide across the lands they visited. The local peoples, inspired by the Atlanteans' wisdom and prowess, sought to emulate their ways, constructing temples and monuments in their honour, and adopting their customs and traditions as a means of drawing closer to the gods who had graced their shores.

But the Atlanteans, for all their size and strength, were not arrogant or tyrannical in their dealings with the local inhabitants. Instead, they sought to uplift and enlighten, to share their knowledge and wisdom with those who were willing to listen and learn. They taught the secrets of agriculture and irrigation, of architecture and engineering, of philosophy and art, guiding the local peoples towards a new dawn of civilization and progress.

And so, the legend of the gigantic Atlanteans, revered as gods by those who beheld them, became intertwined with the history of the lands they visited, From Russia to China and South America to Australia leaving a legacy of wonder that would endure long after their mighty forms had vanished into the mists of time.

Harbour at Atlantis

Titans of Land and Legacy

Chapter 6

In the ancient days of Atlantis, Poseidon, the god of the seas and the master of the realm, gazed upon the central rings of the city with a vision of perfect harmony between water and land. With a deft touch and a divine will, he carved the landscape into a symphony of interconnected canals and waterways, that would come to define the heart of Atlantis.

The central rings of Atlantis, divided equally between water and land, were a marvel of engineering and design. The canals, fed by a network of hot and cold-water springs that bubbled up from the depths of the earth, crisscrossed the city like veins of life-giving energy, bringing sustenance and vitality to every corner of the metropolis. The Atlanteans, with their advanced knowledge of hydraulics and aqueducts, had harnessed the power of water to create a paradise unlike any other in the known world.

But it was not just the waterways that set Atlantis apart—it was also the materials used in the construction of the city itself. The red, black, and white stone quarried locally from the continent of Atlantis formed the foundation of the streets and houses, their vibrant hues lending a sense of grandeur and opulence to the cityscape. The Atlanteans, skilled in the arts of masonry, metallurgy and architecture, had mastered the use of these precious stones to create structures that seemed to rise from the very earth itself, blending seamlessly with the natural beauty of the land.

To encircle the city and protect it from outside threats, not just from warring nations but the wild beasts that roamed in the ancient realm of Atlantis, as the Atlanteans were not the only beings of immense stature, many of the mammals had also evolved to colossal proportions. Within this ancient realm, formidable beasts of breathtaking grandeur and strength roamed, their presence commanding respect and reverence. These majestic creatures, born from the very essence of the primordial world, traversed the lands with a grace and majesty unparalleled by any other living being since the days of the dinosaurs.

The Short-Faced Bear, a titan among predators, strode across the plains like a colossal shadow cast by the setting sun. With a stature that reached the heavens when it stood upon its hind legs 12ft tall, this bear was a symbol of strength and ferocity. Its long legs carried it swiftly across the earth, its slender form a testament to the cunning and agility that made it a masterful hunter of the bison and horses that roamed the lands. Beside the Short-Faced Bear, the Sabre-Toothed

Tiger prowled with a silent grace that belied its immense size and power. Known as Smilodon in the tongue of the ancients, this beast was a creature of primal beauty and deadly intent. With a weight that surpassed 800 pounds, it moved with a fluidity that spoke of centuries of evolution and adaptation to the ways of the land.

Above, the Teratornis bird soared through the skies with wings outstretched like the very fabric of creation itself. Its wingspan, stretching up to 12 feet, cast a shadow over the earth below as it hunted for its prey, with a weight of 176 pounds, it was a behemoth of the heavens,

On the ground, the Mastodons lumbered with a majestic presence Resembling elephants but distinct in their own right, these creatures bore the weight of the world upon their shoulders, their muscled bodies a testament to the strength and endurance that defined their existence.

Powerful workhorses when tamed and amidst them all, the Woolly Mammoths stood as titans, their towering forms reaching up to 13 feet in height and weighing up to 8 tons. Covered in a coat of hair as dark as the night sky, they roamed the lands with a regal dignity that marked them as the kings of the land.

In addition to the awe-inspiring creatures that roamed the lands of Atlantis, there was a colossal Giant Ground Sloth that made its presence known in that ancient realm. Weighing a staggering 8 tons and measuring an impressive 20 feet from head to tail, this majestic sloth stood an imposing 12 feet tall when upright.

In the ancient days of North America, the lakes and wetlands were home to Giant Beavers of astonishing proportions, rivalling the size of black bears in their massive stature. These mega-rodents, weighing approximately 220 pounds, roamed the watery landscapes with a majestic presence.

These creatures and others of immense size, born of the earth and sky, walked the lands of Atlantis with a grace and power that stirred the hearts of all who beheld them. In their presence, the walls of Atlantis stood as a barrier against the untamed forces of nature, protecting the Atlanteans and their kingdom from the wild beasts that roamed their world.

Poseidon ordered the construction of these high walls covered in tin, bronze, and orichalcum—the reddish-golden metal that was more valuable than gold itself. Mined from the many islands that dotted the seas surrounding Atlantis, the orichalcum was brought to the city in carts so heavy that they cut deep track marks in the rock itself, their passage marked by the rumble of the mastodons pulling them towards the harbour with a strength and determination that spoke of the Atlanteans' mastery over the natural world.

As the walls rose higher and higher, gleaming in the sunlight like a barrier of precious metal, the city of Atlantis took on an aura of invincibility and grandeur that struck awe into the hearts of all who beheld it. The combination of water and land, of stone and metal, of nature and artifice, created a city of unparalleled beauty and strength, a testament to the ingenuity and vision of Poseidon and the Atlanteans who had made his dream a reality.

Poseidon, ancient ruler of the seas and lord of Atlantis, gazed across the crystal waters at the empire he had built. The salty breeze carried whispers of time's passage, reminding him that even immortals must eventually yield their earthly domains. His weathered eyes settled upon his ten children, born of his union with the mortal woman Cleito, each bearing the divine spark that marked them as heirs to his vast kingdom.

There stood proud Ampheres, master of the eastern shores, alongside his brother Autochthon, keeper of the fertile valleys. Nearby, Azaes practiced his martial skills, while Diaprepes, known for his diplomatic wisdom, conversed with Elasippus about matters of state. Mestor, the navigator, plotted celestial courses as Mneseus, guardian of ancient knowledge, pored over sacred texts. The youngest four – Eumelus (also known as Gadeirus), Atlas the firstborn, Evaemon the just, and Euaemon the swift – each displayed qualities that would serve their future domains.

As Poseidon watched them, he understood that Atlantis's future lay in their combined strengths. Atlas would rule the central district and capital, as was his birthright, while his siblings would govern the nine outer territories. Each region would reflect its ruler's nature: Ampheres's district would command the eastern ports, Autochthon's lands would feed the nation, and so forth in a carefully balanced arrangement.

Yet the sea god saw beyond mere territorial division. In his divine wisdom, he crafted a system of laws and councils that would bind his children's realms together, ensuring that though divided in governance, Atlantis would remain united in purpose and spirit. Dividing

Atlantis into ten districts, Poseidon appointed each of his children as a king in their respective domain, granting them absolute control over their citizens and laws. However, he imposed a sacred oath upon them—a solemn vow to uphold the teachings and philosophy of Atlantis, to refrain from waging war against each other, and to support one another in times of need. This oath was to be upheld at all costs, ensuring the stability and harmony of the kingdom.

The commands of Poseidon, inscribed on a pillar of orichalcum at the temple of Poseidon in the heart of Atlantis, dictated the order of precedence among the ten kings and regulated their mutual relations. Every fifth and sixth year, the kings would gather at the temple to consult on their common interests, pass judgment on transgressions, and make decisions through a democratic process where the majority ruled.

To seal their oath, the kings engaged in a ritual of great significance. In the temple of Poseidon, they hunted bulls without weapons, capturing a victim to sacrifice over the sacred inscription on the pillar. They swore upon golden cups filled with wine and blood, invoking curses on the disobedient and pledging to abide by the laws of their father Poseidon. They vowed to judge according to the inscriptions on the pillar, to punish transgressors, and to never act against the will of Poseidon as set forth in the sacred texts.

After the ritual, clad in azure robes and gathered around the embers of the sacrifices, the kings deliberated and passed judgments, recording their decisions on golden tablets as memorials of their rule. Special laws were inscribed around the temples, emphasizing the importance of unity, non-aggression among themselves, and coming to the aid of any king whose rule was threatened. The descendants of Atlas were given supremacy in matters of war and governance, and the power of life and death over their kinsmen was subject to the assent of the majority of the ten kings. Thus, the rule of the ten kings of Atlantis was marked by cooperation, democracy, and a shared commitment to the ideals of their father Poseidon. Bound by oath and tradition, they governed with wisdom and fairness, ensuring that the legacy of Atlantis would endure for centuries to come.

Atlanteans With The Megafauna of 12,000 Years Ago

The Edge of Empire

Chapter 7

Many kings had come and gone between Atlas and Tothemak's time, slowly eroding the old philosophy and integrity of the great nation of Atlantis. As the lineage of kings passed over centuries, the once-sturdy foundation of tradition and philosophy began to crumble, giving way to a new era of ambition and desire for power. The age-old values of integrity and harmony, once held sacred, slowly faded into obscurity, overshadowed by the insatiable hunger for dominance that gripped the new rulers of different lands.

The winds of change swept through Atlantis, heralding a new era of uncertainty and discord. The shift in power was palpable, as the once-unified nation found itself divided by the ambitions of its new rulers, whose hunger for dominance knew no bounds. As the shadows of war loomed ever closer. Alliances forged through generations shattered like fragile glass, as loyalty wavered and betrayal lurked in the shadows, waiting to strike at the heart of the kingdom.

The fabric of Atlantis, once woven with threads of unity and strength, now bore the scars of division and strife. The people, torn between loyalty to their heritage and allegiance to the new order, found themselves at a crossroads of conflicting ideals. Greed and aggression seeped into the cracks of society, eroding the bonds that had held them together for centuries.

As the kingdom demanded total dominance over all within its grasp, Whispers carried on the winds from the distant lands of Atlantis, spoke of unrest and rebellion brewing in the hearts of the newly anointed kings, who sought to break free from the shadow of Atlantis and carve their own destinies. No longer content to be subjects of the Atlantean empire, these upstarts yearned for independence and power, their ambitions kindled by the winds of change.

It was during this time that the two brothers, Thothamak and Ozymandias, grew up side by side, in the opulent halls of their ancestral kingdom. Thothamak, the elder of the two, was the rightful king by birth, destined to inherit the throne and the weighty responsibilities that came with it. Yet, from a young age, he displayed a keen intellect and insatiable curiosity that set him apart from his peers.

Ozymandias, the younger brother, was a spirited and ambitious soul, eager to prove himself in the eyes of their people and uphold the legacy of their noble lineage. Despite the difference in their stations, a deep bond of brotherhood and camaraderie flourished between them, forged through shared experiences, laughter, and the trials of youth.

From early on, Thothamak recognized Ozymandias' potential for greatness and wholeheartedly supported his younger brother's aspirations. Knowing that Ozymandias possessed the fire and determination to lead Atlantis to new heights, Thothamak made a pivotal decision to relinquish his claim to the throne, allowing Ozymandias to pursue his ambitions and shape the future of their kingdom.

Driven by a thirst for knowledge and a desire to unravel the mysteries of the world beyond Atlantis, Thothamak delved into the realms of astronomy, metallurgy, philosophy, and cartography. Inspired by the legendary feats of their ancestor Atlas, who had charted the known world centuries before, Thothamak embarked on a quest to continue the legacy of exploration and discovery that which had been lost to the passage of time.

As the brothers stood on the cusp of adulthood, their paths diverged but their bond remained unbreakable. Thothamak's decision to support Ozymandias' journey towards kingship would shape the course of their destinies and set in motion a chain of events that would reverberate across the annals of history.

As the news of these uprisings reached Ozymandias, a fire ignited in his eyes—a fierce determination to quell the dissent and restore order to the distant lands that had dared to defy the authority of Atlantis. The time for decisive action had come, a moment that would test not only his strength and resolve but also the very essence of Atlantean power and prestige in the eyes of the world.

With a steely gaze and a heart set ablaze with the fire of conviction, Ozymandias knew that he must act swiftly and decisively to quell the flames of rebellion before they could spread like wildfire and consume the fragile fabric of the Atlantean empire. The power of Atlantis, forged in the crucible of history and tempered by the trials of time, must be reaffirmed and demonstrated to all who dared to challenge its supremacy.

As Ozymandias gathered his closest advisors in the war room of the Atlantean palace, the flickering torches cast long shadows on the ancient maps spread out before them, marking the vast expanse of the Mediterranean Sea and the lands that bordered its shimmering waters. With a voice that resonated with authority and determination, he outlined his bold plan to quell the uprisings in the distant lands by embarking on a campaign of conquest.

"There are too many distant lands in turmoil for us to quash each uprising individually," Ozymandias declared, "But if we sail our formidable forces around the countries bordering the Mediterranean, reasserting our dominance and reclaiming what is rightfully ours, the echoes of our victories will reverberate across the seas and bring the distant lands back into order."

His advisors exchanged knowing glances, their expressions a mix of apprehension and resolve as they absorbed the weight of Ozymandias' words. The Mediterranean, with its ancient cities and bustling ports, was a strategic gateway to the distant lands that had dared to challenge the might of Atlantis. By dominating the sea routes and reestablishing control over the coastal territories, they would send a clear message to all who dared to defy the authority of the empire.

The plan was audacious, its success hinging on the skill and valour of Atlantean warriors and the strategic genius of their commanders. As Ozymandias laid out the details of the campaign, from the coordinated naval assaults on key ports to the lightning strikes against rebellious strongholds along the coast, a sense of purpose and unity settled over the war room.

Poised on the edge of conquest and glory, Ozymandias and his advisors prepared to unleash the full might of the Atlantean empire upon the shores of the Mediterranean. The clash of swords, the roar of cannons, and the cries of battle would soon echo across the sea, heralding the dawn of a new chapter in the saga of Atlantis—a chapter written in blood and fire, where the empire's power and prestige would be tested as never before.

The stage was set for a confrontation that would shake the foundations of the Atlantean empire to its core, testing the mettle of its rulers and the loyalty of its subjects in a crucible of fire and blood where only the strong and the cunning would emerge victorious. The fate of Atlantis hung in the balance, poised on the edge of a knife, as Ozymandias prepared to make his stand and reclaim the distant lands that had dared to defy the might of the empire.

The legacy of the old kings, tarnished by the actions of their successors, seemed but a distant memory in the face of the impending storm. The people whispered of a time when integrity and respect reigned supreme, a time long forgotten amidst the chaos of the present.

As the sun rose over the majestic city of Atlantis, casting its golden light over the gathered army, a sense of anticipation hung in the air. The ten districts of the empire had mustered their forces, each district contributing its warriors to the grand army assembled to wage war and conquer the lands beyond the Pillars of Hercules. The time had come for Atlantis to extend its reach and dominance over the Mediterranean lands that lay waiting to be claimed.

The leader of the Atlantean army and king, Ozymandias clad in resplendent armour and bearing the mark of his station, oversaw the preparations with a keen eye. It was his duty to furnish the sixth portion of a war-chariot, ensuring that the army would be equipped with a formidable fleet of ten thousand chariots. Each chariot was to be manned by two horses and riders, their steely gazes fixed on the horizon, ready to charge into battle at their leader's command.

In addition to the chariots, the leader was tasked with providing a pair of chariot-horses without a seat, accompanied by a skilled horseman who could fight on foot, carrying a small shield. A charioteer stood behind the man-at-arms, guiding the two horses with precision and skill, ready to unleash their fury upon the enemy ranks.

The army's ranks were further bolstered by two heavy-armed soldiers, their armour gleaming in the sunlight, two archers with bows drawn taut, two slingers poised to let loose a rain of projectiles, three stone-shooters ready to rain destruction upon the enemy, and three javelin-men, light-armed and swift in their movements. To complement the land forces, four sailors were enlisted to man each of the twelve hundred war ships that would carry the Atlantean army to their destined conquest.

Such was the military order of the royal city of Atlantis, a well-oiled machine of war and conquest, honed through generations of discipline and training. While the orders of the other nine governments were to provide equal men and equipment, Atlantis stood as a shining example of military prowess and readiness, poised to sail through the Pillars of Hercules and strike fear into the hearts of all who stood in their path around the Mediterranean.

As the army marched towards the harbour, their footsteps echoing in unison, Ozymandias gazed out towards the horizon. The time for conquest had arrived, and the Atlanteans were ready to unleash the full might of their war machine upon the lands that lay waiting beyond the Pillars of Hercules. Some of the lands had started to have uprisings against the Atlanteans this conquest was to stamp out any resistance once and for all.

As the Atlantean warships set sail from the harbours of Atlantis, cutting through the azure waters with purposeful determination, the air was filled with a mix of anticipation and solemn resolve. The warriors aboard knew that this was no ordinary campaign; it was a journey that would take them away from their homes, their loved ones, and their familiar shores for what could be many long years.

Before departing, they had bid tearful farewells to their wives and children, knowing the hardships and trials that awaited them in the distant lands of the Mediterranean. Some cities would fall easily to the might of the Atlantean army, their defences crumbling in the face of overwhelming force. Others would stand defiant, their walls bristling with spears and their people ready to fight to the last breath.

But regardless of the challenges that lay ahead, the warriors sailed forth with victory and conquest burning brightly in their hearts and minds. They envisioned the spoils of war that awaited them – great treasures, exotic goods, and the glory of vanquishing their enemies in battle. With each passing day at sea, their anticipation grew, fuelling their determination to succeed and return home as heroes.

The journey across the vast expanse of the Atlantic and then the Mediterranean was not without its perils. Storms raged, threatening to capsize the warships and swallow them whole. Yet, the Atlantean sailors, seasoned and skilled, navigated the treacherous waters with unwavering determination, guided by the stars above and the promise of conquest that lay on the horizon.

As they neared the shores of the Mediterranean, the warriors of Atlantis steeled themselves for the trials that awaited them. They knew that some cities would offer fierce resistance, their defenders fighting with a ferocity born of desperation and determination. But the Atlanteans were undaunted, they imagined the celebrations that would greet them upon their homecoming – feasts, songs of victory, and the adulation of their fellow citizens. The thought of such a grand homecoming spurred them onward, driving them to conquer all that lay in their path with a thirst for glory.

Ozymandias With The Atlantean Army

Tide of War

Chapter 8

They sailed past the Pillars of Hercules then on through the straights of Gibraltar, their first target was the rich and ancient lands of Libya then Egypt. With unparalleled speed and precision, their chariots thundered across the vast deserts and fertile plains, carrying well-trained soldiers ready for conquest.

The Atlantean forces struck swiftly, catching the countries of Libya and Egypt off guard with the suddenness of their attack. The cities along the coast fell one by one as the Atlanteans laid siege, their superior tactics and advanced weaponry overpowering any resistance that stood in their way.

Moving inland, and up the rivers the Atlanteans established colonies to solidify their control over the conquered territories. These settlements served as strategic outposts, ensuring that the Atlanteans maintained a firm grip on the lands they had claimed. With each passing day, their influence spread further, and the once-proud nations of Libya and Egypt found themselves under the rule of the Atlantean empire again.

As the Atlantean forces advanced towards the lands of Lebanon, Syria, and Asia Minor, they encountered a different challenge than before. These countries had been forewarned of the Atlantean conquests in Libya and Egypt, and they had prepared themselves for the impending conflict.

The Atlanteans, though skilled and disciplined, faced a formidable resistance from the defenders of Lebanon, Syria, and Asia Minor. The defenders, aware of their foes' tactics and strategies, put up a fierce fight, inflicting losses upon the invaders and slowing down their relentless march of conquest.

To bolster their numbers and overcome the resilient opposition, the Atlanteans enlisted the previously conquered armies to fight alongside them, as the Atlantean forces surged forth like a mighty wave crashing upon the shores of history, they met with both triumph and tribulation in their conquest of the lands surrounding the Mediterranean.

The battles raged across the rugged terrain, from the sun-baked deserts of Syria to the verdant valleys of Lebanon and the coastal plains of Asia Minor, each clash a desperate struggle for survival and freedom. The Atlanteans, with their disciplined ranks and advanced weaponry, pressed forward with relentless determination, their warships dominating the seas and their legions marching inexorably across the land.

But the defenders, inspired by a fierce love of country and a burning desire for liberty, refused to yield without a fight. They waged a guerrilla war of attrition, striking from the shadows and harrying the Atlantean supply lines, inflicting heavy casualties and sowing chaos and confusion in their ranks.

For months, the fate of Syria, Lebanon, and Asia Minor hung in the balance, teetering on the edge of victory or defeat, as the Atlanteans and their adversaries clashed in a deadly dance of death and destruction. The ancient cities of Damascus, Tyre, and Ephesus became battlegrounds soaked in blood and littered with the fallen, their streets echoing with the cries of the wounded and the dying.

In the end, however, the greater force and resources of Atlantis proved too much for the valiant defenders to withstand. Despite their courage and resilience, the nations of Syria, Lebanon, and Asia Minor eventually succumbed to the overwhelming might of the Atlantean empire, their leaders forced to kneel before Ozymandias and swear loyalty to the crown.

The triumph was bittersweet, tempered by the cost in lives and the devastation wrought upon the lands and peoples that had dared to resist the tide of Atlantean conquest. As the sun set on the conquered territories, casting a crimson glow over the shattered remnants of once-proud civilizations, Ozymandias knew that the true test of his rule and the strength of Atlantis lay not in victory, but in the battles and the challenges that would follow and their biggest adversary, the Athenians.

After years of relentless warfare and conquest, the Atlanteans found themselves at the gates of Greece, facing their most formidable adversary yet. These once great allies of Atlantis were now their biggest rivals. The once swift and decisive campaign had stretched into a gruelling seven-year conflict, draining the Atlantean soldiers of their strength and resolve. Despite their weariness, they knew that the final battle awaited them at the heart of Greece, in the illustrious city of Athens.

Slowly advancing along the Greek coast, the Atlanteans encountered fierce resistance from the determined defenders of Greece. The lands surrounding the Mediterranean had been brought under Atlantean control, but the cost had been steep - in lives lost, resources depleted, and time squandered in prolonged warfare.

The Athenians, aware of the Atlantean threat and anticipating the impending siege, had spent six months fortifying their defences and rallying their forces for the ultimate confrontation. The Atlanteans, battle-weary but resolute, now faced an enemy who was not only prepared but also fuelled by a thirst for vengeance against the invaders who had overrun their neighbouring lands.

As the Atlanteans laid siege to Athens, they were met with a united and formidable resistance. Soldiers who had escaped from the conquered territories had joined the Athenian forces, swelling their ranks and bolstering their strength. The Atlanteans were now confronted with a substantial army, driven by a fierce determination to defend their homeland and seek retribution for the suffering inflicted upon their fellow countrymen. The stage was set for a monumental clash between the Atlantean empire and the defiant defenders of Greece, a battle that would determine the fate of nations and the course of history.

As the Atlanteans prepared for the decisive assault on Athens, they mustered their full might and power, assembling a formidable armada of ships whose purpose was to crush the defiant city once and for all. The land army organized its forces into columns of chariot riders, horsemen, and infantry, with skilled bowmen positioned at the rear to provide covering fire over the heads of their comrades.

With a unified command, the Atlantean forces advanced in a synchronized attack from both sea and land, aiming to overwhelm the defenders of Athens. The Athenians, displaying their renowned courage and strategic acumen, positioned their forces outside the city walls, opting to take the battle directly to the Atlanteans rather than await a defensive siege. Embracing the age-old adage that the best defence is a strong offense.

The conflict between Atlantis and Athens was one of epic proportions, a clash of titans that would echo through the annals of history. As the Atlantean armada approached the Athenian fleet, the air was thick with tension and the promise of impending battle. The Athenians, known for their strategic prowess and naval might, prepared themselves for a confrontation that would test the limits of their defences.

The Atlantean fleet was a marvel of engineering and innovation, a testament to the advanced technology and strategic ingenuity that characterized their civilization. Central to their naval dominance were the formidable mega ships, a revolutionary design that had proven devastatingly effective in previous engagements. These vessels were unlike anything the Mediterranean world had seen—a pair of massive triremes joined seamlessly by a sturdy deck, forming a platform for their most fearsome weapon.

Mounted atop this deck was a colossal semi-sphere crafted from orichalcum, a precious metal prized for its resilience and lustre. The surface of the semi-sphere was meticulous, each small panel was slightly angled then highly polished, reflecting the sun's rays with blinding intensity. Ingeniously constructed with flexible joints, the sphere could be angled with precision, allowing the Atlanteans to harness the power of the sun itself as a weapon of war.

As the Atlantean armada closed in on the Athenian ships, they began to manoeuvre into the positions that had brought victory against countless foes. The Athenian sailors, seasoned and battle-hardened, braced for the onslaught, aware of the formidable reputation of their adversaries.

The system the Atlantean mega ships had used was as follows... when they were precisely one stadia from an enemy ship, two triremes that were supporting the mega ships flanked them on either side. These vessels unleashed a relentless barrage of arrows and stones at the enemy ship, forcing their crews to seek refuge beneath their shields. The assault was calculated to confound and distract, leaving the enemy sailors vulnerable and unable to mount a coordinated defence.

With the enemy ship momentarily incapacitated, the Atlantean crew swung into action. The sail covering the semi-sphere atop the mega ship was removed, then the weapon itself was adjusted with meticulous care, its angles calculated to perfection. As the sun's rays converged upon the polished surface, they were focused into a single, searing point of heat, directed at the enemy vessel.

For five tense minutes, the Atlanteans held the semi-sphere in position, the concentrated sunlight beating down on the enemy ship. The effect was both awe-inspiring and terrifying. Flames erupted from the target ship, consuming it in a voracious blaze that left no chance for escape. The once-mighty vessel was reduced to a smouldering wreck, a testament to the destructive power of the Atlantean innovation.

With ruthless efficiency, the Atlanteans shifted their focus to another ship, repeating the process with devastating precision. Ship after ship fell to the inexorable advance of the Atlantean armada, the once-proud fleets of the Mediterranean countries were reduced to a flotilla of burning hulks.

The Mediterranean had never seen a force so formidable, and the legend of the Atlantean mega ships spread like wildfire, striking fear into the hearts of all who dared oppose them. Their mastery of technology and strategy seemed insurmountable, their dominance unchallenged.

As the Atlantean armada unleashed its formidable might upon the Athenian fleet, the air was thick with the acrid smoke of burning ships and the cries of battle. The Atlanteans, confident in their technological superiority and the devastating effectiveness of their mega ships, pressed forward, determined to crush the Athenian resistance.

Yet, the Athenians, renowned for their strategic acumen and adaptability, had not been idle in the face of the Atlantean threat. They had listened to the whispers of the Mediterranean, tales of the Atlanteans' sun-harnessing mega ships. In response, they devised a cunning plan to counter the seemingly invincible Atlantean fleet.

The Athenian navy, drawing upon their ingenuity and resourcefulness, constructed a fleet of specialized battering ships. These vessels were designed with a singular purpose: to neutralize the Atlantean advantage. The bow of each ship was reinforced with a copper coating, a material chosen for its ability to withstand the intense heat of the focused sun rays. This protective layer rendered the Atlantean weapon ineffective, allowing the Athenian ships to close the distance unharmed.

Beneath the waterline, the Athenian ships were equipped with formidable rams, crafted from the same resilient copper. These rams, designed to strike with lethal precision, were positioned to punch through the wooden hulls of the Atlantean mega ships.

As the battle raged, the Athenians launched their counteroffensive. With unwavering resolve, their battering ships charged headlong into the fray, targeting the Atlantean mega ships with fearless determination. The copper-coated prows absorbed the searing heat, allowing the ships to close in on their targets without faltering.

The impact was devastating. The first Athenian battering ship met its mark, driving its copper ram into the side of an Atlantean mega ship. The force of the collision pierced the wooden hull with a shuddering crack, water rushing in as the Atlantean vessel began to list and sink. The crew, caught off guard by the audacity and effectiveness of the Athenian manoeuvre, scrambled to abandon ship.

The Athenians repeated the tactic with relentless efficiency, each successful strike a testament to their ingenuity and tenacity. The balance of power began to shift, the Atlantean fleet now forced to contend with an adversary that had turned their own strengths against them.

As more Atlantean ships were sunk by the determined Athenians, the battle became a more evenly matched contest, a fierce and desperate struggle for supremacy on the high seas. The Athenians, emboldened by their newfound advantage, fought with renewed vigour, determined to defend their homeland and their way of life.

The clash between Atlantis and Athens was no longer a foregone conclusion. What had begun as a display of overwhelming power and technological superiority had transformed into a battle of wits and resilience. The Athenians, driven by their unyielding spirit and strategic brilliance, had turned the tide, proving that even the mightiest of foes could be challenged by those who dared to adapt and innovate.

The clash of arms reverberated across land and sea as the Atlantean ships engaged the Athenian naval defences, while the armies clashed in a fierce and bloody confrontation on the battleground. The battle of Athens became a spectacle of raw power, skilled tactics, and unyielding determination as both sides fought with unmatched ferocity and valour.

The fate of nations hung in the balance as the Atlanteans and Athenians clashed in a titanic struggle that would determine the course of history. The outcome of this monumental battle would shape the destiny of empires and leave an indelible mark on the annals of warfare, marking it as the battle to end all battles.

The Atlantean war machines rolled forward on massive bronze and orichalcum wheels, each one taller than three men. Their intricate spoke patterns were engineered with precise mathematical calculations, allowing the tremendous weight to be distributed evenly across the battlefield. The wheels' rims were studded with cleats that bit into the earth, providing traction as they advanced behind the main assault force. The grinding of their movement created a deep, resonant hum that seemed to vibrate through the very bones of those nearby.

Positioned at the rear of the Atlantean formation, these ten mechanical behemoths were essentially mobile solar furnaces. Their upper sections housed enormous concave mirrors of polished orichalcum, carefully angled to capture and concentrate the sun's rays. The collected solar energy was focused through a network of crystal lenses and amplifiers, creating devastating beams of concentrated light and heat. These rays cut through the battlefield like the spears of gods, clearing paths through the Athenian ranks as Ozymandias led the charge.

The machines worked in perfect coordination, their operators using crystalline signal devices to communicate and synchronize their attacks. As Ozymandias drove forward with his elite guard, the war machines adjusted their positions, their beams sweeping the ground before him like deadly searchlights. The heat was so intense it turned sand to glass and made metal armour glow cherry-red, forcing the Athenian forces to scatter and creating crucial gaps in their defence.

However, the Athenians had studied these machines during previous encounters. They had noticed how the complex mirror arrays needed constant minute adjustments to maintain their deadly focus, and how the crystal amplification systems were vulnerable to sudden shocks. Under the cover of shield formations, they moved their stone-throwers into position, timing their assault perfectly.

The counter-attack came with devastating precision. Multiple stone-throwers launched simultaneously, their projectiles arcing high over the battlefield. The first hits shattered the primary mirrors, sending cascades of broken orichalcum raining down. Secondary hits targeted the crystal arrays, disrupting the entire energy collection system. The machines' deadly beams flickered and died as their systems failed catastrophically.

One by one, the mighty war machines were disabled, their wheels locked, and their weapons silenced. Without the covering fire from their solar weapons, the Atlantean advance was suddenly exposed.

The battle raged on with relentless fury, neither side willing to yield an inch of ground. The air grew thick with the metallic scent of blood and the acrid smoke of burning chariots. Ozymandias's sword flashed like lightning as he parried an Athenian spear thrust, his counterstrike sending the attacker sprawling. But for every Athenian that fell, two more seemed to take their place, their eyes burning with fierce determination to protect their beloved city.

Despite their initial prowess and matched tactics, the tide began to turn. The Athenian phalanx, moving like a single organism, began to push back against the Atlantean advance. Ozymandias watched in growing concern as his war machines began to falter, their crystal cores dimming as Athenian siege weapons found their mark.

In that crucial moment, a coordinated Athenian assault broke through. A skilled Athenian warrior, moving with impossible speed, struck Ozymandias's sword arm with a weighted net, while another knocked his blade free with a well-aimed thrust. The King of Atlantis stumbled, momentarily defenceless, as a wave of Athenian warriors surged forward.

General Theron, seeing his king in peril, spurred his horse through the chaos. With strength born of desperate loyalty, he reached down and grabbed Ozymandias by his armour's shoulder plate, hoisting him onto the back of his mount in one fluid motion. The horse wheeled around, its hooves striking sparks from scattered shields as Theron guided them through the maelstrom of battle. Behind them, the Atlantean lines began to crumble, their ordered retreat deteriorating into a chaotic withdrawal toward their ships.

The sound of defeat - a terrible symphony of breaking formations, desperate shouts, and the triumphant roar of Athenian warriors - followed them as they made their strategic withdrawal. Ozymandias's face was a mask of controlled fury as he watched his grand invasion, years in the planning, dissolve before his eyes. The Athenians, fighting not just for victory but for the preservation of their city and way of life, had proven that their democratic spirit could withstand even the might of Atlantis itself.

As the defeated Atlantean forces boarded their ships and set sail for their distant homeland of Atlantis, a sombre mood hung over the once proud warriors. Ozymandias, the seasoned warrior who had known only victory and glory before this fateful campaign, brooded in silence as the ships sailed homeward. The sting of defeat gnawed at his pride and honour, for this was a setback that cut deep into his very being. The weight of responsibility as the ruler of Atlantis and the commander of its armies bore down heavily upon him, and the bitter taste of failure lingered in his heart.

As the Atlantean fleet sailed back to their island kingdom, Ozymandias grappled with the harsh reality of defeat and the daunting task of facing his people after such a grievous loss. The journey home was fraught with introspection, regret, and a resolve to learn from this experience and emerge stronger than before.

Meanwhile, in the aftermath of the battle, the Athenians tended to the fallen, clearing the battlefield of the dead and offering solace to the wounded. Their victory had come at a cost, but their spirits remained resilient as they turned their attention to rebuilding and healing in the wake of the conflict. The echoes of battle faded into the distance as both sides retreated to reflect on the events that had unfolded and prepare for the uncertain future that lay ahead.

Atlantean Megaship With Orichalcum Heat Weapon

Shadows of Youth

Chapter 9

As Thothamak put the finishing touches on the ancient site of Gobekli Tepe, a place of mystery and wonder that mapped the stars, he received word from Ozymandias that bore grave tidings of defeat and the need for swift action to reclaim lost glory and honour. The war that had begun with such promise had ended in a bitter defeat, leaving Atlantis vulnerable and its ambitions in jeopardy. Ozymandias knew that only by rallying the strength and resolve of his closest kin, his brother who had been engaged in the construction on distant shores, could they hope to turn the tide of fortune and emerge victorious once more.

Thothamak, his mind racing with plans and strategies for even bigger observatories and temples, prepared to depart for Atlantis to meet with Ozymandias, to lend his knowledge and support to the task of rebuilding their shattered forces and preparing for the coming re-engagement with Athens, the last remaining thorn in the side of the Atlantean empire. The Mediterranean lands had been subdued, their peoples brought to heel through conquest and diplomacy, but Athens remained defiant, a beacon of resistance that challenged the authority and power of Atlantis in the region.

Upon his arrival in Atlantis, Thothamak was greeted by Ozymandias, his face grim and determined, his heart set on vengeance and retribution for the losses suffered in the war. The bond of brotherhood that united them, forged in the crucible of adventures and tempered by blood and sacrifice, would be the cornerstone of their efforts to rebuild their armies and reclaim their honour on the battlefield.

Together, the brothers stood before the assembled forces of Atlantis, a sea of faces tired, but ready to follow their leaders into the crucible of war once more. The preparations began in earnest, the training and drilling of troops, the forging of weapons and armour, the gathering of supplies and provisions for the campaign ahead. The time for action was nigh, the moment of reckoning drawing closer with each passing day as the armies of Atlantis mustered their strength and resolved once more to take the battle to Athens and secure their rightful place as masters of the Mediterranean and the world.

Thothamak reminisced about the carefree days of his youth, a memory from their childhood surfaced in his mind like a vivid dream. He recalled a time when he and Ozymandias, still young lads of twelve or thirteen years old and standing a mere six feet tall, had embarked on a daring escapade beyond the walls of Atlantis.

ECHOES OF ATLANTIS, LEGACY OF THE GODS

It was a day like any other, with the sun casting its warm glow over the island kingdom of Atlantis. Under the guise of innocent curiosity and boundless energy, Thothamak and Ozymandias had slipped unnoticed beneath a lumber cart bound for the cedar forests outside the city walls. Despite the warnings of elders about the dangers lurking in the wild beyond the safety of Atlantis, the two adventurous boys saw only the promise of adventure and discovery.

After the cart had deposited its load and rolled away, leaving the boys concealed in the shelter of a large bush, they set out on a quest for the fabled Teratornis bird eggs rumoured to be nestled high on the cliffs of the mountain's edge. The Teratornis, a majestic yet fearsome creature standing 30" tall with a wingspan of over twelve feet, was known to be a formidable predator capable of carrying off small beasts and even unsuspecting infants if they strayed too close.

Undeterred by the tales of danger and driven by youthful bravado, Ozymandias had issued a dare to Thothamak to retrieve one of the prized Teratornis bird eggs. With a mixture of excitement and trepidation, the two brothers ventured forth, their hearts pounding with the thrill of the unknown and the promise of glory that awaited them at the precipice of the cliff.

As they navigated the rugged terrain in search of the elusive eggs, Thothamak and Ozymandias forged a bond that transcended mere blood ties, a bond born of shared adventures and unspoken trust. Little did they know that this childhood escapade would be but the first of many trials they would face together, laying the foundation for the extraordinary paths that lay ahead in their intertwined destinies.

They ventured deeper into the heart of the cedar forest in pursuit of the elusive Teratornis bird eggs, a sudden thrill of excitement coursed through their veins at the sight of the majestic creature soaring high above the treetops. The eerie screech of the Teratornis echoed through the air, sending a shiver down the spines of the young Atlanteans, but instead of fear, a sense of exhilaration filled their hearts as the adventure took an unexpected turn.

With a shared grin and a silent understanding passing between them, Thothamak and Ozymandias pressed forward, their spirits buoyed by the challenge that lay before them. They ascended the tallest cedar tree in the forest, a towering giant reaching over 150 feet into the sky, its branches swaying gently in the breeze like the outstretched arms of a benevolent guardian.

With nimble agility and fearless boldness, the brothers swung from branch to branch, their movements synchronized a combination of daring and skill. As they reached the edge of the cliff, high above the forest floor, a rush of adrenaline fuelled their ascent as they scaled the sheer vertical face of the rock, their fingers finding purchase in the rough surface with practiced ease.

But as they neared a treacherous ledge jutting out from the cliff face, fate intervened with a sudden twist of danger. Ozymandias, his foot slipping on a loose rock, teetered on the brink of disaster, his eyes widening in shock as he felt himself losing his precarious hold on the cliff. In a split-second reaction born of instinct and unwavering loyalty, Thothamak lunged forward, his hand closing around Ozymandias' wrist in a vice-like grip, anchoring his brother to safety and narrowly missing a plunge to certain death. In that fleeting moment of crisis, the bond between the brothers was tested and proven unbreakable. United in their courage and unwavering trust, Thothamak and Ozymandias stood on the precipice of danger, their hearts beating as one in the face of adversity.

As the brothers scrambled up and over the precipice, their hands gripping the rough stone, they found themselves on a narrow shelf of rock that clung precariously to the cliff face. The wind whispered through the crags, carrying the scent of salt and adventure as the brothers inched their way along the treacherous ledge, their eyes scanning the horizon for signs of the unknown.

With hearts pounding and a sense of anticipation building in their chests, they rounded a corner and beheld a cluster of ancient trees standing sentinel at the edge of the cliff. Behind the gnarled trunks and twisted branches, an opening beckoned—a large cave mouth that seemed to swallow the light and echo with the secrets of ages past.

The brothers exchanged a glance, their eyes alight with curiosity and a shared sense of wonder at the discovery that lay before them. The cave, a gaping black window in the belly of the mountain, held the promise of untold mysteries and untamed dangers, drawing them in with a magnetic pull that spoke to the very core of their adventurous spirits.

As they approached the entrance to the cave, the shadows deepened around them, the air growing cool and heavy with the scent of earth and stone. There was a sense of trepidation mingled with excitement as the two adventures stepped over the threshold, their eyes adjusting to the dim interior that stretched out before them like a yawning chasm.

The cave's walls whispered of forgotten tales and ancient echoes, the sound of their footsteps reverberating against the rough-hewn stone like a heartbeat in the depths of the earth. Each step took them further into the unknown, their path illuminated only by the faint glimmer of light filtering in from the entrance behind them.

As Thothamak and Ozymandias ventured deeper into the bowels of the mountain, a sense of excitement and reverence settled over them, mingling with the thrill of discovery and the primal urge to uncover the secrets that lay hidden within the heart of the cave. Little did they know that their journey into the darkness would lead them to the brink of peril.

As they rounded a corner struggling to make their way in the dim light, they beheld a vast cavern stretching out before them, illuminated by a faint glow filtering down from a crevice high above in the ceiling.

The air grew heavy with the scent of rotting and decay, Undeterred by the ominous atmosphere surrounding them, the brothers pressed on, their curiosity driving them forward into the unknown.

As they navigated the winding tunnels that branched off from the main cavern, each passage beckoning with the promise of discovery and danger, a sense of foreboding crept over them. Shadows danced on the walls, casting eerie shapes that seemed to shift and twist with a life of their own, heightening the sense of unease that hung in the air.

But it was when they ducked under a low protruding rock and beheld a pair of gleaming eyes reflecting in the dim light that their courage was truly put to the test. The eyes, glowing with an otherworldly intensity, rose from the ground with an unnatural grace, ascending higher and higher until they hung suspended in the air at a height of over 12ft that dwarfed the two young adventurers.

A guttural roar split the silence, reverberating through the cavern like a thunderclap, as the monstrous form of the short-faced bear emerged from the shadows, its massive bulk poised to strike with lethal speed and primal fury. Realization dawned on Thothamak and Ozymandias as they stood face to face with this apex predator, knowing that their only chance lay in desperate flight.

They raced back through the winding tunnels of the cave, their hearts pounding in sync with the thundering footsteps of the monstrous bear that pursued them, a primal fear gripped their souls. The beast's roars echoed through the labyrinthine passages, its hot breath on their heels as they sprinted towards the faint glimmer of light that marked the exit of the great cavern.

With every stride, every heartbeat, the brothers felt the bear gaining ground, its massive form casting a shadow of dread over their desperate flight. As they burst out of the cave and onto the lip of the cliff, the sheer drop caught them off guard, they knew that their only chance of escape lay in the towering cedar trees that stood fifty feet away and fifty feet below.

Without a moment's hesitation, they launched themselves off the cliff edge towards the swaying branches of the great cedars, their muscles straining with the effort of reaching safety before the monstrous bear could close the gap. The ground trembled beneath them as the beast thundered out of the cave behind them, its enraged snarls and thunderous footsteps driving them to greater speeds and daring feats of agility, their bodies hurtling through the air in a reckless bid for survival. The bear's furious growls reverberated through the forest below, its massive form pacing back and forth along the edge of the cliff as it searched for a way to reach its elusive prey.

As they plummeted towards the forest below, time seemed to slow. The wind whipped past their faces, their hearts pounding in their ears as they reached out with desperate hands toward the approaching canopy. The ancient cedars loomed larger, their branches like welcoming arms in the fading light. The first impact came hard and fast - rough bark scraping against their palms as they grasped at anything within reach. The sharp scent of cedar filled their nostrils as they crashed through the upper branches, needles and twigs whipping their faces.

Branches snapped beneath their weight with sounds like gunshots, each impact sending shockwaves through their bodies. They tumbled through layers of foliage, the world spinning in a kaleidoscope of green and brown. Pine needles showered around them like rain as they bounced from branch to branch, each collision slowing their descent but adding new bruises to their collection. Their clothes caught and tore on stubborn limbs, the forest seeming to grab at them with wooden fingers.

The final plunge through the lower canopy was a chaos of movement and sensation. Smaller branches whipped past their faces, leaving stinging welts across their skin. Their bodies twisted involuntarily, trying to right themselves as the ground rushed up to meet them. Just when it seemed the forest floor would claim them, they crashed through the undergrowth and deflected off a large thicket of mountain laurel and rhododendron.

The resilient bushes bent but didn't break, their springy branches creating a natural crash pad. Leaves and petals exploded around them in a shower of green and pink as they bounced between the sturdy shrubs. The dense network of branches worked like a net, dispersing their momentum through countless points of contact until finally, mercifully, they came to rest in a heap of torn clothes and tangled limbs. Though every muscle screamed in protest and their skin burned from countless scratches, they had emerged from their wild plunge with nothing more serious than bruises and scrapes - a miracle of nature's design and pure luck.

With hearts still pounding and laughter bubbling up from deep within their souls, Thothamak and Ozymandias lay sprawled on the forest floor, gazing up at the dappled sunlight filtering through the canopy above. Relief and joy mingled in their eyes as they realized the gravity-defying feat they had just accomplished, their bodies tingling with the thrill of adventure and the adrenaline of a narrow escape.

Their laughter rang out through the forest, a symphony of shared triumph and unbreakable camaraderie that echoed among the ancient trees and whispered of the countless adventures that had shaped their journey from carefree boys to stalwart young men. Each escapade, each trial and tribulation they had faced together had woven the threads of their bond ever tighter.

From the daring escapades of their youth to the challenges of their passage into adulthood, they had stood side by side, their spirits intertwined through shared experiences and unspoken understanding. Through moments of peril and moments of joy, they had forged a path that led them to this pivotal juncture in their lives, where the past and the present converged in a mixture of memories and dreams yet to be realized.

With a shared chuckle and a knowing glance, Tothamak and Ozymandias decided to postpone their quest for the elusive Teratornis eggs, opting instead for a return to the safety of Atlantis after their heart-pounding encounter with the short-faced bear. The thrill of facing one man-eating monster was adventure enough for the day, and the brothers agreed that discretion was indeed the better part of valour.

As they made their way back through the familiar terrain of the cedar forest, retracing their steps with a newfound sense of caution and respect for the perils that lurked within its depths, the brothers moved with silent grace and swift efficiency. Every rustle of leaves and every whisper of the wind set their senses on edge, attuned to the subtle signs of danger that lay hidden in the shadows.

Stealth became their ally as they navigated the familiar path back to Atlantis, moving with the practiced ease of seasoned adventurers who knew the value of caution and cunning. The forest seemed to whisper its secrets to them, guiding their steps with a silent wisdom that spoke of ages past and untold mysteries.

As they approached the outskirts of Atlantis, the towering spires of the city rising majestically in the distance, the brothers felt a sense of relief wash over them. The familiar sights and sounds of their homeland greeted them like old friends, offering a welcome respite from the dangers of the wild.

Sneaking back into Atlantis through the same hidden route they had used to leave, they moved with the quiet confidence of those who knew the city's every secret and shadow. As they made their way through the bustling streets and winding alleyways, their hearts filled with a mixture of pride and gratitude for the adventures they had shared and the bond that had carried them through every trial and tribulation.

For Thothamak and Ozymandias, the return to Atlantis marked not only the end of one exhilarating chapter but also the beginning of a new phase in their journey, where the lessons learned in the wild would shape their futures and guide them towards the unknown horizons that lay ahead.

As Thothamak regained his thoughts, a heavy burden settled upon his shoulders. Doubt crept into his mind, a feeling of apprehension, as he questioned the wisdom of supporting Ozymandias in his impetuous decisions for Atlantis to re-engage in the war with Athenians.

The legacy of the ancients loomed large in Thothamak's mind, their establishment of trust and trade that had forged a mighty Atlantean empire spanning the known world. Through centuries of diplomacy, friendship, and camaraderie, the Atlanteans had risen to prominence as a beacon of civilization and prosperity, their influence reaching far and wide across the seas and continents.

Yet, in recent times, cracks had begun to form in the once unbreakable unity of the Atlantean empire. Distant kingdoms, swayed by new leaders and ideologies, had started to question the Atlanteans' right to rule, challenging the very foundations of their authority and calling into question the bonds of loyalty and allegiance that had held them together for generations.

Ozymandias' impulsive acts of war, driven by a desire for swift justice and retribution, had now come back to haunt them, casting a dark shadow over the fragile web of alliances and treaties that had sustained the Atlantean empire for so long. The cost of his actions was steep, measured not only in terms of lives lost and resources squandered but also in the erosion of trust and goodwill that had once bound the disparate kingdoms under the banner of Atlantis.

As Thothamak pondered the consequences of Ozymandias' decisions, a sense of unease settled in his heart, mingling with a deep-rooted sense of responsibility and duty towards his people and his homeland. The weight of leadership pressed down upon him, demanding difficult choices and sacrifices that would shape the fate of Atlantis and its people for generations to come.

In the gathering twilight, as the last rays of sunlight faded into darkness and the stars began to twinkle overhead, Tothamak knew that the time for reckoning had come. The fate of Atlantis hung in the balance, teetering on the edge of uncertainty and upheaval, as he grappled with the consequences of his brother's actions and the challenges that lay ahead in the turbulent waters of politics, power, and ambition.

He was about to approach Ozymandias and suggest not a call to war but discretion as the next steps. He knew this would enrage his brother who's only focus was retribution against the Athenians, but he was delayed by a harbinger of doom that would test the very foundations of Ozymandias' rule and the resilience of Atlantis itself.

Thothamak and Ozymandias escaping the shortfaced bear

The Final Warning

Chapter 10

The messenger who brought news of a celestial threat spoke in hushed tones, his eyes wide with fear and disbelief as he recounted the sighting of a comet hurtling through the heavens towards Earth, its path plotted by the great observatory of Atlantis, its new appearance noted in the night sky an indication of catastrophe.

Thothamak, the royal astronomer and keeper of the celestial archives, received the dire tidings with a sinking heart, his mind racing with the implications of this cosmic omen. For generations, the Atlanteans had studied the stars and mapped the movements of the heavens, their knowledge of astronomy and astrology unparalleled in the ancient world. And now, a comet of unknown origin and intent had appeared in the firmament, its trajectory set on a collision course with their world.

The night sky was a canvas of stars, each one a beacon of mystery and wonder. The Atlanteans, had long gazed upward, seeking knowledge in the vastness of the cosmos. Yet, on this night, the heavens had revealed a sinister sign that would shake the very foundations of their civilization.

The news of a new comet in the sky had reached Thothamak with urgency, its implications too significant to ignore. The messenger had spoken of a celestial body, a bright newcomer among the stars, and Thothamak knew he must see it for himself. Without delay, he made his way to the Atlantis Observatory, a sanctuary of learning and exploration perched high above the city.

The observatory was a marvel, equipped with instruments and devices that allowed the Atlanteans to peer into the depths of space with unmatched clarity. As Thothamak entered, the astronomers greeted him with a mixture of excitement and trepidation, aware of the significance of their observations.

They guided him to the viewing platform, pointing to the new light in the night sky. The comet, distant yet undeniably present, shimmered like a jewel against the velvet expanse of the cosmos. The astronomers explained that they had been tracking its movement for two days and were certain it was not a fixed star, but a celestial wanderer on a distinct path.

Thothamak's mind raced as he absorbed the information. He knew that comets had been regarded as omens since time immemorial, harbingers of change or calamity, their appearances recorded in the annals of history. Yet, as he began to calculate its trajectory, a chill settled over him. The numbers told a story of impending doom—a collision course with Earth.

His heart heavy with the weight of this knowledge, Thothamak knew he had to act swiftly. He sought out Ozymandias. Thothamak found him in the great hall, surrounded by advisors and scholars, the air filled with the hum of discourse and debate. He took him to a side chamber so as not to reveal the gravity of the situation to everyone.

"Ozymandias," Thothamak said, his voice grave with urgency. "I bring news of great importance. A new comet has appeared in the heavens, and it is moving with purpose. I have done the calculations, and I fear it is on a collision course with our world."

Ozymandias listened intently, his demeanour calm yet alert, as Thothamak explained the findings of the observatory. The comet, a celestial visitor of unknown origin, posed a threat beyond their control. Even with the advanced technology and knowledge of Atlantis, the power to alter the course of a comet remained beyond their reach. It was, as Thothamak lamented, in the hands of the gods.

"We must prepare," Ozymandias replied, his voice steady with resolve. " The Athenians can wait, though we may not have the power to change the stars, we can ensure that Atlantis is ready to face whatever fate the heavens decree. Let us gather our wisest minds and seek counsel. Together, we shall determine the best course of action."

As the skies were scoured and the observatories trained their lenses on the approaching celestial visitor, the realization dawned that this was no ordinary comet, no mere wanderer in the night sky. Which would give a great demonstration as it sped by, no, its trajectory was too precise, its speed too great, its purpose too ominous to be dismissed. The signs whispered of an impending disaster, of a cataclysm that would shake the very foundations of Atlantis and bring the mightiest empire to its knees.

Thothamak delved into the dusty archives and weathered scrolls of the Atlantean library, seeking answers in the ancient scripts and forgotten lore of his ancestors, he uncovered a chilling revelation that sent shivers down his spine and set his heart pounding with dread. The tales inscribed in the hallowed texts spoke of a great cataclysm that had befallen the world fifty millennia ago, when a comet of unimaginable size and power had struck the land known as Arizona in the distant land of America, wiping out all traces of the civilizations that had come before, erasing the records of the ancestors and leaving only devastation and death in its wake.

The memory of this ancient calamity had faded into myth and legend over the eons, its impact softened by the passage of time and the veil of history that shrouded the past in mystery. But Thothamak knew the truth, for he had beheld with his own eyes the vast crater left by the comet's terrible impact, a scar upon the earth that bore witness to the awesome power of cosmic forces unleashed upon an unsuspecting world.

The parallels between the ancient cataclysm and the approaching comet were too stark to ignore, too ominous to dismiss as mere coincidence. The signs and similarities aligned with uncanny precision, drawing a chilling parallel between the events of the distant past and the looming threat that now menaced Atlantis and all who dwelt within its shining walls.

Thothamak's hands trembled as he traced the faded script and cryptic symbols that foretold of doom and destruction, his mind grappling with the enormity of the knowledge he had unearthed and the implications it held for the fate of the empire. The comet hurtling towards Earth, its fiery descent heralding a repeat of the ancient tragedy that had reshaped the world in ages past, threatened to plunge Atlantis into chaos and despair, to snuff out the light of civilization and consign it to the darkness of oblivion.

With a heavy heart and a soul burdened with foreboding, Thothamak approached Ozymandias and laid bare the grim truth that he had uncovered in the depths of the library's archives. The time had come to confront the echoes of the past, to heed the warnings of history and take action. Atlantis was poised on the brink of annihilation, as the comet drew ever closer, and the hours dwindled towards the moment of reckoning when the skies would once again be rent asunder by the fury of the heavens.

The weight of responsibility settled upon Ozymandias' shoulders, he knew that difficult decisions lay ahead, choices that would determine the fate of Atlantis and its people in the face of the impending cataclysm. With a heavy heart but a resolute mind, he turned to Thothamak, the keeper of ancient knowledge and wisdom, and entrusted him with a crucial mission that held the key to survival in the midst of impending doom.

He was to gather fourteen of the best philosophers and teachers, they would be split into two groups of seven, one for each of the planets. One group travelling East the other group travelling west, they were to take their families with them, and were to restart civilization after this cataclysm, teaching the old ways of Atlantis. Not warfare, but communication, sharing skills and knowledge, and living in peace with each other."

Thothamak felt the gravity of his responsibility settle upon him, but he also sensed the flicker of hope that ignited within his companions. The task was daunting, but it was also an opportunity—a chance to rebuild a world that honoured the values of Atlantis and to right the wrongs that had led to their current predicament.

"Perhaps the gods will be graceful," Thothamak said, "and spare these chosen individuals to put right the wrongs that have been committed recently. It is our duty to ensure that their knowledge and wisdom are preserved and passed on to future generations."

The seven philosophers and teachers of each group would serve as pillars of wisdom, guiding the survivors in rebuilding a society rooted in harmony and enlightenment. It was a chance to create a world where communication and understanding prevailed over conflict and division.

"We must choose wisely," he continued "These individuals will shape the foundation of our new civilization. They should embody the principles of Atlantis and inspire others to do the same."

Ozymandias nodded, appreciating the insight. "Indeed. We will seek out those who have dedicated their lives to learning and teaching, who possess the wisdom and compassion necessary to guide us through this transition."

With that, they began to discuss potential candidates, drawing upon their knowledge of the community. Thothamak felt a sense of urgency; they needed to act swiftly, to gather these pillars of wisdom before the chaos of the world could further unravel their plans.

As they deliberated, Thothamak reflected on the teachings of Atlantis—the emphasis on balance, the pursuit of knowledge, and the belief in the interconnectedness of all life. These were the values that would guide their new society, a beacon of hope in the darkness.

"We'll need representatives from each of the seven planets," Thothamak mused, his mind whirring with possibilities. "Each philosopher or teacher will embody the spirit of their respective celestial body, drawing wisdom from the stars to guide us."

"These are our chosen pillars," Thothamak announced, his voice filled with conviction. "Each one represents the essence of Atlantis, and together, they will teach how to live in harmony with one another and the world around us."

If the gods allowed them to survive, they could re start civilization, returning to the old ways of Atlantis. They were to set sail immediately, the first group were to head west to Peco Duarte a mountain in the Dominican Republic and seek sanctuary there, the other group with Thothamak towards the east and the distant Atlas Mountains, these were both the highest peaks within reach, where hidden caves awaited their arrival—a sanctuary from the impending devastation that threatened to engulf the world.

Ozymandias instructed Thothamak to lead the expedition that was headed east, to go into the depths of a cave in the Atlas Mountains, a place he himself had ventured during an earlier exploration of its labyrinthine tunnels and chambers. Within the bowels of the mountain lay a chance for survival, a glimmer of hope amidst the encroaching darkness that loomed on the horizon.

The philosophers and their families were to travel in secrecy, without alerting the populace to the impending crisis that would spark panic and chaos if word got out. Ozymandias knew that order must be maintained in the face of uncertainty, that leadership and authority were crucial in times of crisis, and that he must remain behind to keep the city calm and prepared for what was to come.

As the philosophers set sail towards the distant mountains, their fate and the fate of Atlantis hanging in the balance, Ozymandias stood alone upon the shores, watching the two ships disappear over their respective horizons, a silent prayer upon his lips for their safety and success in their quest for survival.

The hours stretched into days, the comet drawing ever closer, the skies darkening with foreboding as the people of Atlantis went about their daily lives unaware of the looming threat that hovered above them, waiting to unleash its fury upon the world.

After two days Thothamak, the wise philosopher and leader of his band, stood resolute at the foot of the Atlas Mountains, they had reached them, and he hoped the other group had made it to their mountain sanctuary. A sense of urgency gripping his heart as he surveyed the daunting path that lay ahead. With the imminent cataclysm of the comet hurtling towards them, there was no time to waste in reaching the safety of the cave high up the mountain side before disaster struck. Thothamak knew that it would be a long and arduous race against time, but the survival of his band and the preservation of their knowledge and wisdom depended on their ability to traverse the treacherous terrain and find refuge in the sanctuary of the cave.

Gathering his companions around him, Thothamak outlined the perilous journey that lay before them, emphasizing the need for speed and endurance in the face of the looming threat that hung over their heads like a sword of Damocles. The path ahead was fraught with dangers, from steep cliffs and rocky outcrops to wild beasts and unpredictable weather, but Thothamak was undeterred in his determination to lead his band to safety and secure their future in the face of impending doom.

As they set out on their harrowing trek up the rugged slopes of the Atlas Mountains, Thothamak and his band of philosophers pushed themselves to their limits, their resolve unbroken despite the physical and mental strain of the journey. The sun beat down mercilessly, its rays reflecting off the rocky terrain and sapping their strength with each gruelling step they took towards their goal. Time was of the essence, every moment bringing them closer to the cataclysm that threatened to engulf them in its fiery embrace.

With each passing hour, the sense of urgency grew, the comet blazed across the sky, a portent of destruction and renewal, its fiery tail casting a crimson glow over the landscape as if heralding the end of an era and the dawn of a new age. The earth trembled beneath their feet, the air filled with the scent of impending disaster, but still they pressed on.

They reached the safety of the cave just in time, a sense of relief washed over them like a cool breeze amid a scorching desert. They had provisions to last them a month within the depths of the cave, knowing that they would find a freshwater spring and air vents to ensure their survival in the enclosed space. With the fate of the outside world hanging in the balance and the impending catastrophe of the comet's impact drawing closer by the minute, Thothamak knew that they had made the right decision to seek refuge within the sanctuary of the cave.

Using the full might of his 9ft muscular frame, Thothamak rolled the huge cover stone into position, sealing off the entrance to the cave and blocking out the last vestiges of light that filtered through the opening. The heavy stone served as a barrier against the unknown dangers that lurked outside, protecting them from any wild animals or beasts that might roam the landscape in the wake of the impending catastrophe. With a final heave, he secured it in place, ensuring their safety within the confines of the cave until it was deemed safe to venture out once more.

As the last rays of light faded from view and the darkness of the cave enveloped them in its embrace, Thothamak felt a wave of emotions wash over him, a mixture of solemnity and grief for the world they had left behind and the loved ones they had parted from. He knew that it would not be safe to open the entrance to the cave for at least another few weeks, by which time the world outside would be a drastically different place, forever altered by the cataclysmic event that was about to unfold.

With a heavy heart and tears streaming down his face, Thothamak said a prayer for his brother and his fellow Atlanteans, his voice echoing in the darkness of the cave as he sought solace and guidance in the face of uncertainty and loss, knowing that their survival within the sheltering darkness of the cave was a testament to their resilience and the enduring strength of the human spirit in the face of adversity.

As the echoes of his prayer faded into the silence of the cave, Thothamak and his companions settled in for the long wait ahead, their minds filled with thoughts of the world they had left behind and the challenges that awaited them in the new dawn that would break upon a changed and transformed landscape. Together, they braced themselves for the trials and tribulations that lay ahead, united in their shared resolve to weather the storm and emerge stronger on the other side, ready to face whatever the future held in store for them in the aftermath of the cataclysmic event that would reshape their world forever.

Asteroid Spotted by Astronomers

When Atlantis Fell

Chapter 11

As Ozymandias watched Thothamak's ship disappear over the horizon, a profound sense of loss washed over him like a relentless tide. The realization that he would never see his beloved brother again weighed heavily on his heart, casting a shadow over the once-grand halls of the palace of Poseidon. With a heavy sigh, Ozymandias made his way back to the palace, his mind consumed by memories of shared laughter and shared dreams that now seemed like distant echoes of a bygone era.

Upon his return to the palace of Poseidon, Ozymandias gathered all the servants and courtiers in the grand hall, his voice resonating with a solemn authority that brooked no argument. He informed them that they were free to return home to their loved ones if they so desired, or to take their chances on the open sea in search of a new beginning amidst the chaos that threatened to engulf the world. He thanked them for all the years of great service and hoped some of them would make it through this devastation then they might meet again on the other side. The clock was ticking, with only 24 hours remaining until the comet would strike, leaving devastation in its wake and reshaping the very fabric of existence.

Thothamak, in his wisdom and foresight, had told Ozymandias that he had calculated that the comet would make contact in the north, on the great ice sheets of the cold wastelands where only a few wild beasts roamed. The impact would send shockwaves reverberating across the globe, triggering a chain reaction of cataclysmic events that would alter the course of history forever.

As the hours dwindled away and the comet hurtled closer to its fateful rendezvous with destiny, a sense of urgency gripped the hearts of all who dwelled in the palace of Poseidon. Some chose to heed Ozymandias's decree and set out for the open sea, seeking refuge and redemption in the vast expanse of the unknown. Others remained behind, resigned to their fate and ready to face whatever trials awaited them in the aftermath of the cataclysmic event that loomed on the horizon.

In the final moments before impact, Ozymandias sat resolute on the throne in the palace of Poseidon with his family all around him, his gaze fixed on the darkening sky as the comet descended like a fiery harbinger of destruction. The air crackled with energy, the ground trembled beneath his feet, and a sense of inevitability settled over him like a heavy shroud. With a steady hand and a steely resolve, he braced himself for the impact that would herald the end of an era and the beginning of a new dawn in the turbulent waters of fate.

As the comet made contact with the icy surface of the wastelands, a blinding light filled the sky, illuminating the frozen landscape in a dazzling display of cosmic fury. The impact sent shockwaves rippling across the earth, unleashing a wave of destruction that swept across the land like a vengeful tide. The world quaked and shuddered, its very foundations shaken to the core by the raw power of the celestial visitor that had come to claim its due.

In the wake of the comet's catastrophic impact on the great ice sheets of the north, the once-mighty continent of Atlantis stood on the brink of destruction. The earth trembled and groaned as the comet sliced through miles of thick ice, melting it with ease until it struck the hard earth, sending shockwaves rippling through the core of the planet itself. The result was a cataclysmic chain reaction, triggering massive eruptions of all the volcanoes along the North Atlantic Ridge, the very foundation upon which Atlantis stood. The proud buildings and walls of Atlantis, crafted with expert precision in stone masonry, crumbled like sandcastles in the face of nature's unrelenting fury.

Ozymandias held his family tightly in his arms as the very foundations of Atlantis rocked and shook around them. The palace, once a symbol of strength and grandeur, was now a crumbling edifice, succumbing to the relentless forces of nature. The walls trembled violently, sending dust and debris cascading from the ceilings, while the statues of his ancestors—those proud representations of a lineage steeped in wisdom and valour—fell one by one, shattering into pieces that echoed the despair of a civilization in its final moments.

They sought refuge in the holy chapel, the heart of Atlantis, revered for its strength and sanctity. It had stood firm against the chaos that had unfolded, its walls steeped in prayers and blessings that once protected the people. But even this sacred space, where countless generations had gathered to seek guidance and solace, was not immune to the cataclysm that had befallen them. Though the ancient stones had withstood the violent tremors that shattered the earth beneath their feet, a far greater threat loomed. As they survived the initial force of the earthquake that ravaged Atlantis, none could have predicted the devastating chain of events that followed.

The comet's impact in the northern realms had unleashed forces beyond comprehension. The sky itself had turned to fire, as superheated debris rained down across thousands of miles. Massive pressure waves rippled through the atmosphere, creating storms unlike anything seen in human memory. The impact sent plumes of vaporized ice sheet high into the stratosphere, where it condensed and fell as scalding rain across entire continents. The very air became thick with ash and steam, turning day to night.

The tremendous energy of the collision instantly liquefied vast sections of the ancient ice sheets, releasing millions of years of trapped water in mere moments. The impact crater itself became a massive cauldron, where molten rock met ice in an explosive contest that sent shockwaves through the earth's crust. These seismic disturbances triggered fault lines across the globe, awakening long-dormant volcanoes and splitting open new fissures in the ocean floor.

Now, a wall of water taller than the highest towers of their civilization rushed toward them with unstoppable force, carrying with it the combined fury of displaced oceans and melted ice sheets. The tsunami approached with such speed and magnitude that even their most sacred sanctuary would soon be nothing more than another secret for the sea to claim.

As the tsunami approached, a low roar filled the air, a harbinger of the impending doom that would wash away everything they had ever known. Ozymandias felt the ground beneath him tremble as the chapel began to sway. The ornate gold and silver ornaments, once a testament to the wealth and artistry of their civilization, flew through the air like projectiles, colliding with the walls and shattering into fragments.

Panic surged through him as he glanced at his family, their faces pale with fear and uncertainty. He could see the vulnerability in their eyes, a reflection of the chaos that surrounded them, and his heart ached for the safety and security he could no longer provide.

"Stay close to me," he urged, his voice steady despite the turmoil. "We will face this together."

As the waves of the tsunami crashed against the walls of the chapel, the sound was deafening—a monstrous roar that drowned out all other noise. The water surged forward, a wall of destruction that swept through the palace, consuming everything in its path. Ozymandias held his family closer, their bodies pressed together as he prepared for the inevitable, the final embrace of life and love amidst the chaos.

In that fleeting moment, time seemed to stand still. Memories flooded his mind—laughter shared around the dinner table, stories told by candlelight, the warmth of their love that had filled the halls of the palace. He thought of his ancestors, the legacy they had built, the dreams they had nurtured, and the hope that had flourished amidst the challenges they faced. All of it flashed before him, a bittersweet reminder of what had been and what would soon be lost.

As the chapel was engulfed by the rushing waters, Ozymandias felt the familiar tug of despair, but he also felt an overwhelming sense of love for his family. He closed his eyes, surrendering to the moment, hoping that somehow, in the depths of the chaos, they would find a way to survive, to endure, and to carry forth the legacy of Atlantis even as the world around them crumbled.

The wave struck with unrelenting force, tearing through the chapel and ripping it from its foundation. The water surged into the sacred space, swirling around them like a tempest, and for a brief moment, Ozymandias felt weightless, suspended between life and death. As the current pulled them away, he held his family tighter, willing the strength of their bond to withstand the tempest that sought to tear them apart.

In the depths of the abyss, as the light faded and darkness enveloped them, Ozymandias clung to the last vestiges of hope. He whispered words of love and reassurance to his family, knowing that even in the face of annihilation, their spirits would endure. The legacy of Atlantis would not be silenced by the fury of nature; it would echo through the ages, a testament to the resilience of the human spirit and the unbreakable bonds of love that transcended time and space.

The earth convulsed beneath their feet, the inhabitants of Atlantis were thrown into chaos and despair. The once-stable ground quivered and heaved, cracking open like a gaping wound as the force of the impact reverberated through the land. Buildings swayed precariously; their stone foundations tested beyond their limits as the very fabric of reality seemed to unravel before their eyes. Panic and fear gripped the hearts of the Atlanteans as they struggled to make sense of the devastation unfolding around them, their world crumbling like a fragile dream in the wake of nature's wrath.

With a deafening roar, the great city of Atlantis began to crumble, its towering spires and majestic structures reduced to rubble in a matter of moments. The once-proud walls that had stood for centuries now lay shattered and broken, a testament to the impermanence of even the mightiest civilizations in the face of Mother Nature's unforgiving power. The Atlanteans watched in disbelief as their home was torn asunder, their lives upended in an instant as they faced the harsh reality of their own mortality.

The boiling lava, unleashed from its ancient prison beneath the ice caps, erupted with a ferocity that defied imagination. The sea of molten rock surged through the thin surface of the earth, propelling hundreds of feet into the air before cascading down upon the hapless population of Atlantis. There was no escape, no shelter from the scorching rain of fire and destruction that engulfed the once-proud city. Buildings that had managed to withstand the initial shockwave now became engulfed in flames, adding to the chaos and devastation that had turned Atlantis into a living hell on earth.

During the inferno, the people of Atlantis faced a choice - to succumb to despair or to fight for survival with every fibre of their being. Families were torn apart, loved ones lost in the merciless deluge of lava and flames that consumed everything in its path. Amidst the screams of agony and the crackling of burning buildings, a sense of desperate resolve took hold as the survivors banded together, seeking whatever refuge they could find amid the devastation. The very air they breathed was thick with ash and despair, but still, they clung to hope, a flickering flame in the darkness that refused to be extinguished.

A wave of destruction swept across the once-verdant lands of Atlantis, transforming them into a desolate wasteland of ash and ruin. The skies darkened with ash and smoke, blocking out the sun and casting a pall of darkness over the shattered remnants of the once-great continent. The fury of nature knew no bounds, its wrath unleashed with a ferocity that left no stone unturned and no soul untouched by its devastating embrace.

As if the Atlanteans hadn't faced enough devastation, the worst was yet to come. The aftermath of the comet's cataclysmic impact was not merely a tale of lava and fire; it was a prelude to chaos that would shake the very foundations of their existence. The massive heat generated from the comet's collision had melted so much of the great ice sheet that it unleashed a monstrous tsunami—a force of nature that no one could have prepared for. This was no ordinary wave; it towered over 200 feet high, traveling at incredible speeds across the ocean with an insatiable hunger for destruction.

The warning signs were subtle at first—a slight tremor beneath their feet, a distant rumble that reverberated through the air, The water pulled back from the white-sand beaches like a massive inhalation, exposing the seabed in a way never before witnessed. The normal gentle slope of the shoreline transformed into a vast expanse of glistening wet sand stretching out nearly a mile into what should have been ocean.

Stranded fish flopped desperately in newly formed pools, while beached ships lay helplessly tilted on their sides. The exposed ocean floor revealed a graveyard of lost items - ancient artifacts, weathered timbers, scattered coins gleaming in the sunlight. Steam rose from underwater volcanic vents newly exposed to the air.

In the city, people gathered at the grand harbour walls, pointing and shouting at the unprecedented sight. Some, understanding the deadly omen, were already running toward higher ground. The great bronze gates of the harbour stood useless, defending against an absent sea.

On the horizon, a dark line appeared - barely visible at first. It grew steadily taller, a wall of blue-black water that seemed to touch the clouds. The sound came next - a deep roar like distant thunder that grew into the rumble of a thousand charging bulls.

The water began flowing back, first as small streams and rivulets across the exposed seabed, then faster, racing toward the city as if drawn by the approaching wave. Ships crashed against each other as the water returned. The tsunami now stood as tall as the highest temples, blocking out the sun and casting a dark shadow over the panicking city. then the very coastline but soon, the horizon began to darken as the wave approached, a monumental wall of water fuelled by the energy of the melting ice. The sky turned ominously grey, and a cacophony of sound filled the air as the tsunami drew closer, a deafening roar that drowned out the cries of the people who had already endured so much.

The survivors of Atlantis, still reeling from the aftermath of the cataclysm, had little time to react. Many stood frozen in shock, their eyes wide with disbelief as they turned to face the approaching wall of water. Panic set in as they realized the futility of escape; there was no place to run, no refuge to seek. The wild animals and beasts that roamed the land were caught in the same fate, their instincts failing them against the sheer magnitude of the wave that would sweep away everything in its path.

As the tsunami crashed upon the shores of Atlantis, it consumed the land with a ferocity that was unimaginable. The power of the wave surged forward, filled with debris, rocks, and remnants of the once-great civilization. Buildings that had stood proud moments before were swept away like mere toys, the very essence of Atlantis engulfed in a relentless torrent of destruction. The ocean, now a raging beast, churned violently, grotesque in its fury as it took back what had once been its own.

The survivors, those few who had managed to endure the fires and eruptions, were now met with the ultimate test of their resilience. The tsunami struck with a thunderous crash, and the force of the water was overwhelming. Those who were still standing found themselves swept away in an instant, swallowed by the depths of the churning sea. The echoes of their cries were drowned out by the roar of the ocean, a haunting symphony of despair that reverberated through the landscape.

The aftermath of the comet's impact had left the great continent of Atlantis in a state of irreversible transformation. The once-mighty land, revered for its towering structures and flourishing cities, was now buried beneath a thick layer of volcanic rock—a molten legacy of the fury that had been unleashed. The combination of the lava that had erupted from the depths below, coupled with the immense weight of the ice that had melted away, created a perfect storm of geological upheaval. The earth itself began to shift and sink, as the mountains that had once stood proudly were forced into the void left behind by their own destruction.

As the lava cooled and solidified, it formed an inescapable blanket over the ruins of Atlantis, sealing the fate of the civilization that had thrived there for millennia. The coastal towns and cities, once vibrant with life, now lay submerged beneath the rising waters, victims of the tsunami's wrath and the subsequent elevation of sea levels that left no refuge. The ocean, now a vast and indifferent expanse, claimed what had once belonged to the land, forever altering the geography and legacy of the great continent and the world.

Asteroid Impacting The Ice Sheet

Sanctuary in Shadow

Chapter 12

In the depths of the ocean, the remnants of Atlantis lay still, shrouded in darkness and mystery. The once-bustling streets, adorned with intricate mosaics and vibrant markets, were now silent. Schools of fish swam through the ruins, weaving in and out of crumbled archways and eroded statues, as nature began to reclaim what humanity had built. The echoes of laughter and life faded into a haunting silence, the memories of a civilization lost to time. their beauty hidden beneath layers of sediment and saltwater slowly entombed in a carcase of mud.

Thothamak and his fellow survivors huddled in the dim light of the enclosed cave, oblivious to what was about to happen to Atlantis, the echoes of their whispers mingling with the distant sounds of dripping water. Since they had blocked themselves in, they could only imagine the chaos that would consume Atlantis, their sanctuary both a blessing and a curse. The cave offered them shelter from the devastation outside, yet it also felt like a prison, its stone walls closing in around them with just a flickering torch to light their way.

The anxiety in the air was unmistakable, a mixture of eagerness and dread. The survivors were torn between the desire to escape their subterranean refuge and the fear of what awaited them in the outside world. They had heard strange sounds of creatures in flight some even trying to break the stone door down to seek refuge themselves.

Then there had been a deafening roar that filled the air, shaking the very ground beneath them. The survivors froze, their hearts racing as they instinctively turned their gazes upward. The great comet, a blazing harbinger of destruction, streaked across the sky, its fiery tail illuminating the heavens with an otherworldly glow and lighting up the entire cave. The sound was unlike anything they had ever experienced, a deep rumble that resonated within their bones, echoing the cosmic cataclysm that had sealed their fate.

Then came the collision—a thunderous crash that reverberated through the very fabric of the earth, a sound that hadn't been heard since the dinosaurs were wiped from the pages of history. It was a moment that transcended time, a reminder of the fragility of existence and the power of nature to reshape the world in an instant.

Thothamak's heart raced as he instinctively drew his companions closer, their eyes wide with terror and wonder. The sound of the impact was a terrifying reminder of what all their fellow Atlanteans were about to face, they felt guilty for being so far away locked in their safe haven, knowing the rest of their family and friends were experiencing unimaginable horrors, wrought by this harbinger of death. They all embraced each other in silence, tears streaming down their face's eyes locked shut as if to block out the images they were all imagining.

Just as Thothamak and the survivors began to find solace huddled together, the ground beneath them suddenly trembled. It was a low, ominous rumble that sent a jolt of fear through the group, causing them to scream in terror and their hearts to race. Before they could comprehend the source of the disturbance, the shockwave hit their mountain hideaway with a violent intensity, as if the very earth itself was shaking in response to the cataclysmic forces unleashed upon the world.

The entire mountain range seemed to shift, the rocks groaning and cracking in protest as the shockwave poured into the cave through the crevice gaps. Dust and debris filled the air, swirling around them like a tempest. Thothamak struggled to maintain his balance, and he felt the ground shift beneath his feet, knocking some of his companions off balance and sending them sprawling to the floor.

Panic surged through the survivors as they scrambled to regain their footing amidst the chaos. The cave walls trembled, and stones tumbled from above, crashing to the ground like thunderclaps. Thothamak reached out to steady a young woman who had fallen, pulling her back to her feet. Her eyes were wide with terror, but he could see a flicker of determination within them.

"Stay focused!" he urged, glancing around at the others. "We need to move deeper into the cave!"

As the shockwave continued to reverberate through the mountain, the survivors clung to one another, their hearts pounding in unison. The very foundation of their sanctuary felt as though it might collapse at any moment, and the urgency of their situation began to sink in. They had thought they had escaped the worst of the destruction, only to find themselves facing yet another peril.

Thothamak led the group deeper into the cave, navigating the winding passages with urgency. The sound of rumbling rocks and the distant echoes of the world outside filled the air, a constant reminder of the chaos that had unfolded beyond their shelter. They needed to find safety before their haven became their tomb.

Suddenly, the tremors intensified, and a deafening roar echoed through the cave, drowning out all other sound. Thothamak stumbled forward, nearly losing his footing once more, but he pressed on, urging his fellow survivors to follow him. The cave seemed to be alive, pulsating with energy as they navigated the twisting tunnels downwards.

As Thothamak and his companions continued their descent deeper into the tunnels, the air grew cooler, and the sounds of the outside world faded into a distant memory. The flickering flames of their makeshift torches illuminated the walls, revealing intricate patterns etched into the stone, remnants of a time long forgotten. Each step they took echoed in the stillness, a reminder of their solitude in the heart of the mountain.

Eventually, they came upon a gigantic chasm that seemed to stretch endlessly into the depths below. The sheer magnitude of the void left them breathless, and they paused to take in the sight before them. Stalactites hung from the ceiling like the fangs of a great beast, glistening with moisture that caught the light of their torches and cast shimmering reflections on the stone walls. The beauty of the underground cavern was overwhelming, a hidden world that felt both wondrous and foreboding.

Thothamak stood at the edge of the chasm, gazing into the abyss. "It's incredible," he breathed, his voice barely above a whisper. "This place... it's like a cathedral of stone."

The others gathered around, their faces illuminated by the flickering light. They felt a moment of peace wash over them, a brief respite from the chaos that had consumed their lives. Here, in this hidden sanctuary, they could momentarily forget the horrors of the outside world and embrace the beauty that surrounded them.

As they settled on the rocky ground, the group took a moment to catch their breath and share their thoughts. The tension that had built within them during their harrowing escape began to dissipate, replaced by a sense of camaraderie that had been forged in the fires of adversity.

But as they rested, Thothamak couldn't shake the feeling that their time in the cavern was limited. The flickering lights of their torches were beginning to fade, the flames struggling to maintain their strength in the damp air. He glanced around at his companions, noting the weariness etched on their faces and he knew they needed to conserve their energy.

"We can't stay here for too long," he said, breaking the silence. "We must move forward before our lights go out completely. The darkness can be a treacherous companion."

The others nodded in agreement. They had come too far to turn back now, with renewed purpose, they rose to their feet and cautiously approached the edge of the chasm. The sound of dripping water echoed through the cavern, a reminder of the life that thrived even in the darkest of places. Peering into the depths, they could see the faint glimmer of water reflecting the light from their torches, a sign that there was still movement beneath the surface.

Thothamak turned to his companions, gesturing towards a narrow ledge that appeared to wrap around the chasm. "We can traverse that ledge. It may lead us to another passage."

One by one, they stepped onto the ledge, their hearts pounding as they carefully navigated the rocky outcropping. The chasm yawned below them, and the darkness felt alive, as if it were beckoning them closer to its depths. But with each step, they felt the bond of trust and determination strengthen between them.

As they made their way along the ledge, Thothamak's thoughts drifted to Atlantis. He wondered how his brother Ozymandias was, had he managed to escape? Was there anything left of Atlantis? He could feel his brother urging him to be brave, to seek the light even in the darkest of times. They had built a civilization that thrived on knowledge and innovation, and he realized that it was now his responsibility to carry that legacy forward.

After what felt like an eternity of cautious steps, they finally reached a point where the ledge widened, revealing a small alcove. The flickering light of their torches illuminated the space, revealing ancient carvings on the walls that depicted stories of exploration and triumph. It was a reminder of the strength and resilience of their ancestors, a beacon of hope in the darkness.

"This place is a treasure," one of the survivors exclaimed, his eyes shining with excitement. "Look at the artistry! These stories... they speak of our history!"

Thothamak felt a surge of pride as he examined the carvings. "This is a testament to who we are," he said, his voice filled with conviction. "We carry their legacy within us. We must learn from their wisdom and carry it into our future."

As they rested in the alcove, the last flickers of their torches began to fade, but the light of hope burned brightly within them. With hearts united and spirits unyielding, Thothamak and his companions prepared to continue their journey. They would navigate the depths of the chasm, seeking a way to rise from the ashes of their past and carve a new path forward in a world forever changed. The darkness may have threatened them, but together, they would find the light that would guide them home.

Thothamak led his companions deeper into the cavern, their spirits buoyed by the discoveries they had made. The salty breeze that began to fill the air was both unexpected and exhilarating, a reminder that they were not as far removed from the world above as they had originally thought. As they pressed on, the scent of the ocean grew stronger, mingling with the earthy aroma of the damp stone. It spurred a flicker of hope within him, urging him to discover its source.

Following the gentle pull of the breeze, they approached a wall that appeared to have been partially obscured by a pile of rocks and debris. Thothamak felt a surge of determination as he examined the obstructions.

"There might be an opening beyond this wall," he said, turning to his companions. "Let's clear this rubble and see what lies beyond."

With a collective nod, they set to work, each person lending their strength to the task at hand. They dug and pushed, sweat beading on their brows as they cleared away the rocks that had been piled against the wall. The effort was arduous, and fatigue began to set in, but the promise of the salty breeze and the distant sound of water kept their morale high.

As they worked together, cracks of light began to appear through the gaps in the rocks. Thothamak's heart raced at the sight—each beam of light felt like a thread of hope pulling them closer to freedom. With renewed vigour, they redoubled their efforts, digging deeper and pushing harder against the stones that had kept them confined.

Finally, after what felt like an eternity, the last of the rocks tumbled away, revealing a narrow passageway that led to a cliff edge overlooking a vast expanse of water. The sight took their breath away. The cave opened to a magnificent view—a shimmering ocean that stretched endlessly to the horizon, its waves crashing against the jagged rocks below.

Thothamak stepped closer to the edge, the salty breeze now enveloping him, filling his lungs with the scent of freedom, his companions joined him on the cliff face, the vast expanse of the Atlantic Ocean stretched out before them. The water sparkled like a million diamonds, its rhythmic waves crashing against the rocky shore below. For a moment, the beauty of the scene offered a sense of peace, a fleeting reminder of the world they once knew. But as they took in the serene vista, the skies above told a different story.

In the distance, a mighty pillar of ash rose into the atmosphere, an ominous column that loomed like a dark cloud over the horizon. It billowed skyward, swelling into a monstrous shape that resembled a nuclear explosion, but it was ten times larger and more terrifying. Thothamak's heart sank as he recognized the source—this was the aftermath of the comet that had struck Atlantis, a cataclysmic event that had altered the very fabric of their world.

"Look at that," one of the survivors breathed, pointing toward the ominous plume. "What has happened to our home?"

Thothamak squinted against the light, his heart heavy with dread. "It appears the comet did not just strike the surface; it unleashed a devastation we cannot yet comprehend. The ash cloud is a sign of destruction on an unimaginable scale."

The others fell silent, their faces reflecting a mixture of horror and disbelief. They had known the comet would cause great upheaval, but witnessing the magnitude of the devastation from such a distance was a stark reminder of the fragility of their existence. Atlantis had once been a beacon of civilization, filled with knowledge and culture, and now it lay shrouded in darkness.

Then Thothamak squinted into the distance, trying to comprehend what he was seeing. The ocean, once a serene and inviting expanse, now appeared to rise ominously into the sky as if it were a colossal wall of water ready to crash down upon them. The sight was both awe-inspiring and terrifying, a reminder of the unpredictable forces of nature that had already ravaged their world.

"My God," Thothamak exclaimed, his heart racing. "A tsunami! Quick, back inside! Head up the tunnels; we may be high enough, but we're not taking any chances! Move as fast as you can!"

The urgency in his voice echoed through the group, and without hesitation, they turned on their heels and sprinted back towards the cavern entrance. Adrenaline coursed through their veins as they retraced their steps, the earlier sense of wonder now eclipsed by a new fear closing in around them.

The rocky ledges that had once filled them with excitement now felt treacherous beneath their feet. Thothamak urged his companions to keep moving, their breaths coming in quick gasps as they navigated the narrow passages. The sound of the crashing waves intensified, a deafening roar that reverberated through the tunnels, amplifying their sense of urgency.

"Keep going!" Thothamak shouted,

Glancing back at the chasm opening. The wall of water loomed closer, its height a terrifying testament to nature's fury. The salty breeze that had once invigorated them now felt like a warning, a prelude to the chaos that awaited.

They hurried inside, the sounds of their footsteps echoing against the stone walls. The once-comforting shadows now felt oppressive, and the thought of being trapped within the mountain filled Thothamak with a sense of dread.

As they moved deeper into the tunnels, he could feel the vibrations of the impending tsunami reverberate through the ground beneath them. The air grew thick with tension, and he could see the fear in his companions' eyes as they pressed forward, driven by the instinct to survive.

"Find a place to brace yourselves!" Thothamak commanded,

his voice firm despite the chaos surrounding them. They reached the wide chamber, its high ceiling offering a sense of safety, and he directed them to huddle together, using their bodies to shield one another.

"We need to stay together and stay low."

The sound of the ocean crashing against the cliffs grew louder, a monstrous roar that threatened to drown them in its fury. Thothamak closed his eyes for a moment, focusing on the strength of his companions around him. They had faced so much together already, and he knew that their bond would be their greatest asset in the face of impending doom.

When the first wave hit, it was like a thunderclap, a force that shook the very foundation of the mountain. Dust and debris rained down from the ceiling, and some of the stalactites came crashing down, the ground trembled beneath them as if the mountain itself were alive. Thothamak clenched his jaw, bracing himself against the wall, his heart pounding in rhythm with the chaos outside.

"Hold on!" he shouted, his voice barely audible over the cacophony. "We will survive this! We are strong!"

As the second wave struck, the sound was deafening, a roar that engulfed them completely. The water surged upward, crashing against the cliffs and sending tremors rippling through the tunnels. Thothamak felt the weight of uncertainty pressing down on him, but he refused to let fear take hold. He focused on the faces of his companions, their expressions a mixture of fear and determination, and he took a deep breath, channelling their collective strength.

Time seemed to stretch as they huddled together, the world outside becoming a blur of sound and fury. In that moment, he realized that their survival depended not just on the physical space they occupied but, on the unity, they had forged in their journey. They were more than just individuals fighting for their lives; they were a family bound by shared experiences and resilience.

With adrenaline coursing through their veins, Thothamak and his fellow survivors charged toward the narrow passage leading away from the chasm. The roar of the ocean reverberated behind them, a chilling reminder of the tsunami that had surged through their world. They could feel the water gushing into the tunnels, the air pressure building ominously, and the urgency to escape was unmistakable.

"Keep moving! Don't look back!" Thothamak shouted,

His voice cutting through the chaos as they sprinted forward. The sound of rushing water echoed in their ears, drowning out everything else, but the instinct to survive propelled them onward.

Just as they cleared the threshold of the tunnel, a deafening crack split the air. Thothamak glanced up in horror to see a massive stalactite, dislodged by the force of the incoming pressure, plummeting towards them. Time seemed to slow as the rock fell, and he felt a surge of panic as he realized the danger they were in.

"Run!" he yelled,

urging his companions to push forward as they ducked beneath the archway of the tunnel. With one last desperate leap, they made it through just as the stalactite came crashing down behind them.

The impact reverberated through the ground, and plummeting fragments filled the air, obscuring their vision. Thothamak stumbled but regained his footing, turning to see the stalactite had sealed the tunnel behind them, blocking the rising water from following. Though they were now trapped within the confines of the mountain, they had narrowly escaped certain doom.

"Keep moving! We can head back the way we came. Hopefully, the passages and tunnels won't be blocked, and we can get back out the way we got in!" Thothamak urged,

his voice steady despite the uncertainty that loomed around them. The group had lost their torches in the chaos of the tsunami, and now they found themselves plunged into pitch blackness. The darkness pressed in on them, thick and suffocating, but Thothamak knew they couldn't afford to panic. They had to stay focused, to rely on their instincts and the bond they had forged through their shared trials.

"Stay close together," he instructed, feeling the cool stone of the wall beneath his fingertips as he led the way. The air was damp and heavy, carrying the faint scent of salt and earth. He strained his ears, listening for any signs of the water that had threatened to consume them, but the silence was unnerving.

"Is everyone still with us?" he asked,

turning to the sounds of shuffling behind him. The muffled responses reassured him; they were still a unit, still navigating the unknown together. As they moved deeper into the darkness, memories of the journey they had taken began to swirl in Thothamak's mind. The strength of their camaraderie. They had faced insurmountable odds before—this was just another chapter in their story.

"Remember the carvings we saw?" one of the survivors whispered, trying to break the silence. "The stories of those who overcame great challenges? We're part of that legacy

Thothamak nodded, feeling a sense of pride swell within him.

"Exactly. We carry their strength with us. We must believe in ourselves and each other."

He continued to guide them through the darkness, relying on his memory of the twists and turns they had taken during their descent. He felt the walls shift beneath his hands, the passageways narrowing and widening as they moved forward. Each step was a reminder that they were not lost; they were merely in the midst of a trial that would ultimately lead them to safety.

After what felt like an eternity of navigating the dark tunnels, Thothamak noticed a faint glimmer of light in the distance. Hope surged within him, and he quickened his pace.

"There's light ahead!" he exclaimed, his voice breaking the silence with renewed energy. "We're getting closer!"

The group instinctively moved faster, the promise of light drawing them nearer. As they approached, the faint glow grew brighter, illuminating the rough stone walls around them. The sound of dripping water echoed in the distance, a reminder that they were still underground but no longer engulfed by the oppressive darkness.

"Let's take a moment to regroup," Thothamak suggested, his mind racing with possibilities. "We can use the light from this chamber to guide us back through the tunnels. We'll retrace our steps and find a way to the surface."

As they gathered their strength, Thothamak felt a renewed sense of purpose. They had faced the darkness together, and now they would face the light.

"Ready?" Thothamak asked, looking around at his companions. They nodded; their expressions determined. "Let's move forward."

Thothamak led the group, his heart steady as they retraced their earlier path. The air felt fresher, as they maneuvered through the twists and turns, Thothamak felt the bond between them strengthen. They were no longer just a group of survivors; they were a family. The darkness had tested them, but they had emerged resilient and determined to reclaim their lives. Eventually, they reached a familiar passage, and Thothamak felt a surge of hope as they approached the cave.

"Just a little further," he encouraged, urging them onward. "We can do this!"

With renewed determination, they pressed forward, then among the litter of rocks and debris, he spotted something familiar—some of their belongings that they had left behind during their hasty descent into the mountain.

"Look!" he called out, beckoning to his companions. "Some of our things! We've made it back!"

His voice echoed with a mixture of excitement and disbelief. In the chaos of their escape, they had abandoned many essentials—packs of food, blankets, and some of their treasured belongings. These items had once been a part of their journey, and now they represented a connection to their past, a reminder of the life they had fought so hard to preserve.

After gathering their possessions and taking a moment to absorb the enormity of the ash cloud rising in the distance, Thothamak turned to face his companions. He could see the weariness etched on their faces, the toll that their harrowing journey had taken. They had faced the unknown, braved the darkness, and were now in a world that was forever changed. It was time to pause, and to take stock of their situation.

"We'll rest here," Thothamak declared, his voice steady and reassuring. "Who knows what other dangers the comet will throw our way? We have our supplies, which will see us through, and I believe this is the safest place to stay for now."

His words hung in the air, a promise of respite amidst the turmoil. The survivors nodded in agreement, their bodies sagging with exhaustion but their spirits still alight with hope. Thothamak could sense that they needed this moment—a chance to catch their breath, to reflect on what they had endured, and to prepare for the challenges that lay ahead.

"We can wait it out for a week before venturing outside to see what is left of the world we knew," he continued, his eyes scanning the horizon. "This cave offers us shelter from the elements, and we can set up camp here. Together, we will plan our next steps."

As they began to unpack their supplies, the atmosphere shifted from one of tension to a sense of camaraderie. The act of settling in, of creating a small haven amidst the chaos, provided a sense of normalcy that had been sorely lacking. Thothamak watched as his companions worked together, their laughter mingling with the sound of the ocean waves lapping against the rocks below.

Tsunami Consuming Atlantis

When Giants Fell

Chapter 13

After a week of being sealed within the confines of the cave, Thothamak's thoughts were consumed by the world beyond. The days had passed in a quiet, almost surreal stillness, marked only by the soft whispers of his companions and the gentle flicker of firelight that cast dancing shadows on the cave walls. The oppressive silence from outside had been both a comfort and a source of unease, suggesting that the chaos they had fled from might have finally subsided.

But the lack of sound from the world beyond the stone—no birdsong, no rustling of leaves, no distant calls of animals—filled Thothamak with apprehension. He knew they could not remain hidden forever, that they needed to assess the state of the world outside and determine their next steps. The prospect of confronting the unknown was daunting, yet necessary.

As he rose from his resting place, Thothamak felt the weight of his decision. His companions watched him with a mixture of anticipation and anxiety, their expressions mirroring his own trepidation. They had survived the darkness together, but now they faced a new challenge—the uncertainty of a world forever altered by the comet's wrath.

"We need to see what's become of the outside," Thothamak said, his voice steady but tinged with concern. "It's been silent for too long. We must find out what awaits us beyond these walls."

He approached the stone that had sealed their refuge, the barrier that had protected them from the chaos beyond. The memory of rolling it into place was still fresh in his mind—the effort it had taken, the relief of knowing they were safe inside. But now, it was time to reverse that act, to open the door to whatever lay beyond.

Thothamak placed his hands on the cool, rough surface of the stone, feeling its weight beneath his fingers. It was a formidable obstacle, but one he had overcome once before. He took a deep breath, summoning the resolve that had carried them through their trials.

"I'll need help to move it," he said, turning to his companions. "Together, we'll open the way."

Without hesitation, they joined him, forming a line around the stone. Their collective strength had brought them this far, and Thothamak knew it would see them through this moment as well. He felt the warmth of their unity, their shared determination to face whatever awaited them outside.

"On three," Thothamak instructed, his voice firm. "One... two... three!"

With a concerted effort, they pushed against the stone, muscles tensing as they strained against its weight. For a moment, it seemed immovable, a reminder of the safety it had provided. But slowly, it began to shift, the grinding of stone against stone echoing in the confined space.

As the stone rolled aside, fresh air rushed into the cave, carrying with it the scent of the sea and the earth. It was a breath of freedom, a promise of the world that lay beyond. Thothamak felt his heart quicken, a mixture of fear and excitement coursing through him.

The opening revealed a sliver of light, a glimpse of the outside world that beckoned them forward. Thothamak peered through the gap, his eyes adjusting to the brightness after days of darkness. He could see the rocky expanse of the cliff face, the ocean stretching out beyond, and the ominous ash cloud which had now spread throughout the sky a testament to the cataclysm that had reshaped their world.

With their path cleared, they moved cautiously toward the entrance, their hearts filled with a mixture of hope and trepidation. The world beyond awaited them, a landscape both familiar and foreign, shaped by forces beyond their control.

As they emerged from the cave, the grey sun light seemed alien even in its warm glow, a reminder of the resilience of life and the promise of renewal but also a great change had taken place. Thothamak felt a sense of determination settle over him. They had weathered the storm, and now they would face the future with courage and unity.

The path down the mountain lay ahead, a descent into the heart of a landscape forever altered by the cataclysm. As they began their journey, the enormity of the change that had swept over their world became increasingly apparent.

The mountain tops and hills retained their majestic silhouettes against the sky, offering a semblance of continuity in a world disrupted. The rocky terrain beneath their feet felt solid and reassuring, a reminder of the earth's enduring presence. Yet, as they made their way downward, the view that unfolded before them was one of profound transformation.

The sea, once a distant horizon, now encroached upon the land with an unfamiliar intimacy. It had risen over 100 feet, its vast expanse swallowing the coastline that had been their home. The familiar contours of the shore were gone, replaced by a watery landscape that blurred the boundaries between earth and sea.

Thothamak paused, taking in the scene with a mixture of wonder and sorrow. The tops of trees jutted out from the water, their leafy crowns swaying gently with the movement of the waves. It was as if half the land had been swallowed by the ocean, a testament to the power of the natural forces that had reshaped their reality.

"It's hard to comprehend," one of his companions murmured, her voice tinged with disbelief. "Everything we knew… it's beneath the waves now."

Thothamak nodded, his heart heavy with the weight of loss. The world they had known, the places they had cherished, were submerged beneath the sea, hidden from view but not forgotten. Yet amidst the devastation, there was a strange beauty to the scene—a reminder that life persisted, even in the face of overwhelming change.

As Thothamak and his companions reached the water's edge, the vastness of the transformed landscape stretched before them, a daunting expanse with no clear paths or roads to guide their way. The familiar markers that had once defined their world were now either submerged beneath the waves or buried beneath mud and debris, leaving them to navigate the unknown with only their instincts and the remnants of their memories.

The silence that hung over the altered land was deafening – gone were the thunderous footfalls of the great mammoth herds that once shook the earth as they passed, their massive forms no longer darkening the horizon like moving mountains. The mighty mastodons that had cleared paths through the densest forests had vanished, along with the fearsome sabre-toothed tigers that had stalked the grasslands.

Where once the colossal Teratornis birds had ruled the skies with their twenty-foot wingspans, casting great shadows over the plains, now only smaller scavengers circled above. The rich tapestry of megafauna that had defined their world had been torn asunder – the giant ground sloths, the towering cave bears, the fierce dire wolves – all seemed to have vanished in the wake of the great catastrophe. Thothamak thought he had glimpsed what might have been a small group of mammoths trudging through the distant haze, a few scattered survivors among the great beasts, these were mere shadows of the vast herds that had once roamed freely across the continents.

He thought their disappearance would be profound and far-reaching. He imagined what would happen to the great grasslands, once maintained by the constant grazing of mammoth herds, they would begin to transform. Without these massive browsers to keep the vegetation in check, the landscape would start shifting – woody shrubs invading the prairies, and forest boundaries beginning to creep outward. The paths that these giants had carved through the forests, which had served as natural corridors for countless other species, would begin to close.

The loss of the apex predators – the sabre-toothed cats, dire wolves, and short-faced bears – would allow smaller predators to multiply unchecked. The intricate balance that had existed for millennia was unravelling. The great beasts had been nature's gardeners and architects, their very presence shaping the land itself. Their dung had fertilized vast areas, their footprints had created microhabitats for smaller creatures, and their browsing had maintained the mosaic of different habitats that supported such diverse life.

He thought this was the end of an era, not only had the great Atlanteans, those magnificent beings who towered 12 feet in the air, been possibly wiped from the earth, but all the other great-sized mammals that had slowly evolved into their majestic proportions since the time of the dinosaurs were now facing extinction. These creatures had grown steadily larger over millions of years, reaching their zenith just before this catastrophe struck. The megafauna had achieved their massive size through eons of adaptation, surviving countless climate shifts and challenges, only to face this sudden, insurmountable threat.

The Atlanteans themselves had represented the peak of human potential for size and strength, their civilization built on the shoulders of giants. But nature's pattern of gigantism hadn't been limited to them – it had expressed itself across countless species. The cave bears had grown to enormous size, the dire wolves dwarfed their modern cousins, and even the humble beaver had reached the size of a modern bear in its form called Castoroides.

But now, Thothamak realized, the age of giants was ending. The catastrophe had broken the evolutionary ladder that had led to such magnificent sizes. The survivors would be the smaller, more adaptable species – the ones that could hide in burrows, survive on less food, and reproduce quickly. The next age would belong to the quick and modest-sized – the deer instead of the mammoth, the wolf instead of the dire wolf, the regular-sized humans instead of the mighty Atlanteans.

He understood that this was more than just a disaster – it was an evolutionary reset, a great levelling that would force life to begin anew from a humbler starting point. The future would favour those who could adapt to a world with less abundance, where being small and efficient would prove more advantageous than being large and powerful. The age of giants had been magnificent, but it had also made them vulnerable – their great size requiring vast amounts of food and making them unable to hide from catastrophe.

Thothamak stood at the edge of the newly formed coastline, his gaze sweeping across the horizon. The absence of familiar landmarks and wildlife was unsettling, and a sense of uncertainty settled over the group. But amidst the confusion, Thothamak recalled a fragment of the past that might guide them forward.

"There used to be a harbour just around the cove," he said, his voice steady with determination. "If we are lucky, we may find something we'll be able to adapt into a makeshift boat."

His companions exchanged hopeful glances, the prospect of finding a means of transportation igniting a spark of possibility. The notion of a harbour, a place where vessels once gathered and set forth on journeys across the sea, offered a glimmer of direction in a world that seemed to have lost its bearings.

Together, they began to make their way through the debris, the dense foliage a testament to the transformation that had swept over the land. The path was overgrown and uncharted, but each step brought them closer to the cove that lay just beyond the bend.

As they rounded the curve, the scene that unfolded before them was one of both devastation and hope. Debris was strewn along the newly formed coastline, remnants of a world that had been torn apart by the fury of the tsunami. Broken planks, tangled ropes, and shattered remnants of once-sturdy structures littered the shore.

But amidst the wreckage, Thothamak's keen eye caught sight of something miraculous—a few boats, battered but intact, had survived the worst of the storm. They lay nestled among the debris, their hulls weathered but remarkably repairable.

"Look!" one of his companions exclaimed, pointing toward the boats. "We might be able to use those!"

A surge of relief washed over Thothamak as he assessed the vessels. They were small and worn, but they held the promise of mobility, a chance to explore the new world that lay beyond the horizon. Each boat represented an opportunity, a vessel of hope that could carry them forward.

"We can repair these," Thothamak said, his voice filled with determination. "With some work, they will serve us well. We can use them to navigate the waters, to find others, and to begin rebuilding."

The group moved toward the boats with renewed energy, their hands eager to set to work. They scavenged the debris for materials—planks for patching, ropes for securing, and sails that could be repurposed. Thothamak guided their efforts, his years of experience as a navigator and builder coming to the fore.

As they toiled under the sun, the rhythmic sounds of their labour mingled with the gentle lapping of the waves against the shore. It was a symphony of creation, a testament to their resilience and resourcefulness. With each plank they nailed into place, each seam they sealed, they were not just repairing boats—they were forging a path forward, reclaiming their legacy as explorers and builders.

The work was hard and the hours long, but the promise of the open sea spurred them on. Thothamak felt a sense of camaraderie among his companions, a shared purpose that bound them together in their quest. They were not just survivors; they were pioneers, carving out a future in a world that had been forever changed.

As the sun dipped toward the horizon, casting a warm glow across the water, the boats began to take shape. Their hulls were patched, their sails rigged, and their masts stood tall against the sky. Thothamak surveyed their work with pride, his heart swelling with hope.

With their boats now seaworthy and their spirits buoyed by the prospect of discovery, Thothamak and his companions boarded their vessels, ready to set forth into the vast unknown. The newly risen shore had provided them with a bounty of scavenged goods—food, tools, and other essentials that would sustain them on their journey. It was a testament to their resilience and adaptability, a reminder that even in the face of devastation, they could find a way forward.

As they pushed off from the shore, the salty sea breeze filled their sails, and the boats began to glide smoothly across the water. The daylight revealed a world that was both familiar and alien, with the once-recognizable coastline now transformed beyond recognition. The landmarks they had relied upon had vanished beneath the waves, leaving them to navigate this altered landscape with only their instincts and the stars to guide them.

Thothamak stood at the helm, his hands firm on the wheel as he steered their course. He felt a pang of disorientation—a reminder that the world they had known was gone, replaced by a new reality that defied their expectations.

"It's hard to find our way during the day," one of his companions remarked, "Everything looks so different now."

Thothamak nodded, understanding the challenge that lay before them. The landscape had changed, the sea had risen, and the familiar markers that had once guided their journeys were nowhere to be found. But he knew that, in time, they would learn to read the signs of this new world, to find their way through its mysteries and uncover its secrets.

As the day gave way to night, the sky transformed into a canvas of twinkling stars, each one a beacon of hope in the darkness. Thothamak felt a sense of calm wash over him, the familiar constellations offering a comforting reminder of the universe's constancy. This was his favourite time to steer, when the world seemed to shrink away, and all that remained was the vast expanse of the ocean and the guiding light of the stars.

Under the cover of night, Thothamak could almost forget what had happened—the cataclysm that had reshaped their lives, the loss of Atlantis and all it had represented. In the stillness of the night, it was as if time had paused, allowing him to navigate by the same celestial patterns that had guided his ancestors for generations.

"The stars are unchanged," Thothamak mused aloud, his voice carrying across the deck to his companions. "They remind us of who we are and where we come from. As long as we have the stars, we will find our way."

His companions gathered around, their faces illuminated by the gentle glow of starlight. There was a sense of unity among them, a shared belief in the power of the cosmos to guide their journey. They were explorers, navigating a world in flux, yet anchored by the eternal presence of the stars.

As the boats sailed through the night, Thothamak felt a renewed sense of purpose. The ocean stretched out before them, a vast expanse filled with both danger and promise. It was a new frontier, a canvas upon which they could paint the future of their civilization.

As the two ships hugged the altered coastline, Thothamak kept a vigilant eye on the horizon, his mind focused on the task of navigation. The dawn light began to creep over the edge of the world, bathing the sea in hues of gold and amber. With the first rays of morning, Thothamak felt a renewed sense of purpose, his instincts as a navigator sharpening as he sought to regain his bearings.

For generations, the Pillars of Hercules had been a steadfast landmark, standing tall against the sky as a gateway to the Mediterranean Sea. These two towering rock formations, each rising 100 feet into the air, had marked the narrow entrance to the Mediterranean lands, guiding countless mariners through the shallow opening and into the heart of ancient civilizations.

But now, as Thothamak scanned the horizon, a sense of unease settled over him. The familiar silhouette of the Pillars was nowhere to be seen. The sea had risen, swallowing the landmarks beneath its waves, transforming the once-narrow passage into a vast, uncharted expanse of water.

"The Pillars should be visible by now," Thothamak murmured, his voice tinged with disbelief. "We're nearing their location, but there's nothing on the horizon."

His companions exchanged concerned glances, the absence of the Pillars a stark reminder of the changes that had reshaped their world. The entrance to the Mediterranean, once clearly marked and easily navigable, was now an open sea—a daunting expanse with no visible markers to guide their course.

"It's as if the gateway has vanished," one of his companions remarked, peering into the distance. "The sea has swallowed it whole."

Thothamak nodded, his heart heavy with the realization. The Pillars of Hercules, a symbol of strength and endurance, had succumbed to the ocean's relentless rise. The gateway to the Mediterranean was no longer defined by towering rocks but by the boundless water that stretched before them.

Determined to uncover the fate of their homeland, Thothamak made the decision to alter their course. Though the Pillars of Hercules no longer stood as guiding beacons, he was confident in his ability to navigate by the hilltops that flanked the entrance to the Mediterranean Sea. With a steady hand and a heart full of resolve, he steered the ships back toward where Atlantis had once stood—a place rich with history, wisdom, and memories.

Thothamak Viewing The Devastation After The Tsunami

Sea of Memories

Chapter 14

The journey was fraught with anticipation and uncertainty, each mile bringing them closer to the truth of what had become of their beloved Atlantis. As they sailed onward, a dark expanse began to unfold across the horizon, creeping over the ocean like an ominous shroud. Thothamak and his companions watched in bewilderment, the sight unlike anything they had ever encountered.

"What is it?" one of his companions asked, her voice a mix of awe and dread. "It looks like a shadow cast over the sea."

Thothamak narrowed his eyes, studying the unusual phenomenon. As they drew closer, the nature of the dark expanse became clear—it was thick mud, a disconcerting amalgam of volcanic pumice stones, ash from the cataclysm, and the remnants of countless islands that had been swept away by the sea.

"This must be the aftermath of the destruction," Thothamak said, his voice laced with sorrow. "The ash and debris from the volcanoes have coalesced into this impenetrable barrier."

For two days, they attempted to navigate through or around the thick mud, their ships struggling against the oppressive mass that coated the ocean's surface. The once-clear waters were now a morass of grey and black, the air heavy with the scent of earth and decay. Progress was slow and arduous, and each passing hour whittled away at their hope.

"We can't get through," another companion remarked, frustration evident in his tone. "It's like the sea has turned against us."

Thothamak's heart ached at the realization. The homeland they sought was beyond reach, hidden beneath a sickening blanket of mud that stretched as far as the eye could see. The great mountains of Atlantis, which should have been visible even from this distance, were nowhere to be found. The horizon was obscured, the landscape transformed into a monochrome expanse devoid of life.

"Atlantis is buried beneath this," Thothamak said quietly, the weight of the loss settling over him. "What was once our home, our sanctuary, is now entombed under this veil of ash and mud."

The ships came to a standstill, their crews grappling with the enormity of what lay before them. The realization was a bitter pill to swallow—their beloved homeland, with its towering spires and verdant fields, was gone, swallowed by the forces of nature and time.

The afternoon sun hung low in the sky, casting long shadows over the lifeless expanse of mud and debris that stretched before them. Thothamak and his companions stood at the edge of this transformed world, their hearts heavy with the weight of loss and the stark reality of the devastation that had claimed their homeland. Despite their hopes of finding some type of life, the scene remained unchanged—silent, still, and devoid of life.

As Thothamak gazed across the desolate seascape, his thoughts turned inward to the faces and voices of those who had been lost to the cataclysm. Ozymandias, his brother and guide, who had entrusted him with the task of preserving the wisdom of Atlantis. His family and friends, whose laughter and love had filled the halls of their once-vibrant city. All were now gone, consumed by the forces that had reshaped their world.

"There is nothing we can do now," Thothamak said quietly, his voice barely rising above the gentle lapping of the waves against the hull of the ship. "We must accept what has happened and honour those we have lost."

His companions gathered around, sharing in the collective grief that bound them together. The loss was immeasurable, but so too was the depth of their love and the strength of their resolve to carry forward the legacy of Atlantis.

"We will send blessings to all our beloved ones who have passed over," Thothamak continued, his voice filled with a solemn reverence. "Tonight, we hold a vigil in memory of them all."

As the sun dipped below the horizon, casting the sea in twilight hues, the survivors prepared for their vigil. They lit candles on the decks of their ships, the flickering flames casting a warm glow that pierced the encroaching darkness. The gentle sound of the ocean accompanied their quiet prayers, a fitting tribute to those who had been lost.

Together, they formed a circle, their hands joined in a gesture of unity and remembrance. Thothamak led them in a moment of silence, each person reflecting on the lives that had touched theirs and the memories they would carry forward. The air was filled with a sense of peace, a gentle acknowledgment of the past and a promise to honour it through their actions.

The vigil stretched into the night, the stars overhead bearing witness to their tribute. It was a moment of purification, a chance to release their grief and embrace the future with renewed determination. Though the path ahead was uncertain, they were fortified by the spirit of those they had loved and lost.

As the first light of dawn began to break, casting the world in a soft golden glow, Thothamak felt a sense of renewal settle over him. The vigil had been a turning point, a chance to honour the past while embracing the promise of the future. The journey ahead was daunting, but they were ready to face it together.

"At dawn, we head for the Mediterranean lands," Thothamak announced, his voice filled with quiet resolve. "We will see what we can find there, and we will forge a new beginning for ourselves and the legacy of Atlantis."

As Thothamak and his companions charted their course back toward the Mediterranean, a sense of uncertainty lingered in the air. The landscape they had once known so intimately was forever altered, a testament to the power of the cataclysm that had reshaped their world. With each passing mile, the realization grew stronger: nothing that was before would ever be the same again.

Their ships sailed through the open waters, guided by the rising sun and the promise of new beginnings. As they approached the location where the Pillars of Hercules should have stood, Thothamak felt a pang of disbelief. The narrow channel that had once marked the entrance to the Mediterranean Sea was now a wide expanse of water, the iconic rock formations swallowed by the relentless rise of the sea.

"How could so much change in such a short time?" Thothamak murmured to himself,
struggling to comprehend the enormity of the transformation. The sea had claimed the land with a ferocity that defied understanding, reshaping the very geography of their world.

His companions shared in his astonishment, their expressions a mix of wonder and sorrow. The landmarks that had guided their ancestors for generations were gone, leaving them to navigate a world that was both familiar and foreign. Yet, despite the loss, they pressed onward, driven by the hope of discovering what lay beyond the horizon.

As they passed through the widened expanse where the Pillars should have been, the realization of their new reality settled over them.

The Mediterranean stretched out before them, a vast sea filled with history and potential, waiting to be explored and understood.

Their journey continued, the ships cutting gracefully through the water as they headed toward the coastline where the first city should have been. It was a place rich with history, a bastion of culture and commerce that had thrived for centuries. But as they approached, the sight that greeted them was one of emptiness and desolation.

The city was gone, its streets and structures submerged beneath the waves. There was no sign of life, no remnants of the bustling port that had once been a hub of activity. The sea had claimed it all, leaving only a silent blanket of water in its wake.

Thothamak's heart ached at the sight, the loss of the city a stark reminder of the impermanence of all things. The civilization that had flourished along the coast was now a memory, preserved only in the hearts of those who had called it home.

The journey continued along the Mediterranean coast, with Thothamak and his companions passing the once-thriving ports and harbours of Libya, now eerily silent and submerged. The coastline, which had been a bustling hub of trade and culture, lay in ruins, a testament to the devastation that had swept through the region. Despite the loss, they sailed close to the shore, hoping to find some sign of life amidst the debris.

The sight that greeted them was one of desolation. The remnants of buildings, shattered and broken, were strewn along the coastline, a stark reminder of the force that had wrought such destruction. The harbours were gone, their docks and piers swallowed by the sea.

"There's no one left," one of Thothamak's companions observed, her voice filled with sorrow. "The ports, the cities—they're all gone."

Thothamak nodded, his heart heavy with the weight of loss. He had once walked these shores, marvelled at the architectural wonders that had lined the coast, and contributed to the construction of grand edifices that spoke to the ingenuity and creativity of their civilization. Now, all were submerged beneath the waves, their grandeur hidden from view but not forgotten.

As they sailed on, they came upon a river that had not existed before—a new waterway carved by the force of the tsunami, its banks lined with debris. Thothamak felt a pang of recognition, remembering a favourite town that had once stood by a small stream in this very location. It had been a place of respite and community, a haven where he had often stopped during his travels.

"This must have been where the town stood," Thothamak said, pointing toward the river's mouth. "The stream is gone, replaced by this new river. The tsunami must have swept everything away."

The realization was a bitter pill to swallow. The town, like so many others, had been annihilated by the relentless force of nature, its buildings and people consumed by the waves. Thothamak thought of the friends he had made there, the memories he had cherished, and felt a deep sense of loss for a world that had been irrevocably changed.

As they sailed up the river, the realization of the scale of the devastation became increasingly clear. The landscape was unfamiliar, reshaped by the waters that had surged through, erasing the past and leaving only echoes of what once was.

"We can't dwell on what's gone," Thothamak said, his voice filled with determination. "We must focus on what lies ahead. We can rebuild, create new communities, and honour the legacy of those we've lost."

With the river behind them, they returned to the open sea, their ships cutting through the water. The Mediterranean stretched out before them, Though the past was lost, the future lay open, waiting to be shaped by their hands.

As the ships continued their journey across the Mediterranean, Thothamak stood at the helm, his thoughts focused on the path ahead. The decision to sail to Egypt had come with a sense of purpose, a determination to find a place where they could begin anew. Egypt, with its rich history and enduring legacy, seemed the ideal destination—a land where the promise of renewal could take root amidst the echoes of the past.

"Our supplies will get us to Egypt," Thothamak assured his companions, his voice steady with conviction. "That is where we will start again. There, amidst the remnants of what once was, we will find a way to help and rebuild."

His companions gathered around. The journey had been long and fraught with challenges, but the prospect of reaching Egypt filled them with a renewed sense of purpose. It was a land that had withstood the test of time, a place where they hoped to find some resemblance of the life they had known before the cataclysm.

"I'm sure there will be some semblance of the life we knew somewhere in this great land," Thothamak continued, his gaze fixed on the horizon. "Egypt has always been a beacon of civilization, and it is there that we will lay the foundations for the future."

In his bag, Thothamak carried the tablets of the fourteen Atlantean laws, a precious legacy entrusted to him by Ozymandias. These laws, etched in stone, encapsulated the wisdom and principles that had guided their society for millennia. They were a testament to the values of peace, knowledge, and unity that had defined Atlantis—a legacy that Thothamak was determined to uphold.

"With the tablets, we will reestablish and build what our ancestors did thousands of years ago," Thothamak declared, his voice filled with resolve. "We will create a society that reflects the true spirit of Atlantis, free from the greed that began to seep into our world."

His companions nodded in agreement, their eyes reflecting the same determination. The Atlantean laws were more than just words; they were a blueprint for a harmonious society, a guide to creating a world where knowledge and compassion prevailed over power and greed.

As the ships sailed onward, the anticipation of reaching Egypt grew with each passing day. The land of the pharaohs was a place of enduring mystery and grandeur, a civilization that had stood the test of time.

Thothamak felt a deep connection to this ancient land, a sense that it was here, amidst the pyramids and the Nile, that they would find the strength to rebuild.

His mind flashed to the ancient scrolls he'd studied - records of his ancestor Mneseus, who had stood alongside Egypt's first king as they established Memphis. That great city of knowledge, where countless historical records were preserved in vast libraries, where the wisdom of ages was carved in stone and written on papyrus. His ancestor had helped build those first archives, ensuring the preservation of humanity's earliest memories.

The journey was long, but the promise of Egypt sustained them. The Mediterranean, vast and filled with history, lay behind them, while the future beckoned from the shores of a land that had witnessed the rise and fall of countless empires.

Holding A Vigil In The Muddy Sea

Legacy in Stone

Chapter 15

As they approached the coast of Egypt, the sight of the land filled them with awe and hope. The Nile, a lifeline of fertility and abundance, flowed with the promise of renewal.

"This is where we begin anew," Thothamak said, his voice filled with quiet reverence. "Here, in Egypt, we will honour the legacy of Atlantis and create a future that is worthy of our past."

As the ships sailed along the coast of Libya and approached the land of Egypt, Thothamak felt a stirring of anticipation and nostalgia. Egypt had always held a special place in his heart, a land where he had left an indelible mark with his architectural prowess. The Nile, a source of life and inspiration, had provided the setting for some of his most ambitious creations, structures that stood as testaments to the ingenuity and artistry of a bygone era.

Thothamak's mind was filled with memories of the countless hours spent designing and overseeing the construction of these megalithic masterpieces. Each building was a monument to human achievement, carved with explicit detail from gigantic granite stones. The structures had been designed to withstand the passage of time, their grandeur intended to inspire awe and reverence for generations to come.

As they neared the Egyptian coast, Thothamak scanned the horizon with bated breath, hoping to catch a glimpse of the monuments he had crafted with such care. The knowledge that some of his creations might have survived the cataclysm filled him with a sense of hope and longing.

"Egypt is where I poured my heart and soul into my work," Thothamak said, addressing his companions as they drew nearer to the shore. "I've built many structures around the world, but here, along the Nile, are some of my greatest achievements. I hope they have endured."

His companions listened intently, sharing in his anticipation. The prospect of seeing the legacy of Thothamak's work—structures that had stood as symbols of human achievement and resilience—was a beacon of hope amidst the uncertainty that had defined their journey.

As they sailed further into the Nile delta, the landscape began to reveal the traces of a civilization that had flourished for millennia. These monumental structures, built by the hands of countless skilled artisans, were a testament to the skill and vision of those who had come before.

"There," Thothamak exclaimed, pointing toward a cluster of structures along the riverbank. "Those are the buildings I designed—these ones have survived."

As the ships navigated the waters of the Nile, Thothamak's eyes were drawn to a familiar silhouette on the horizon—a structure that filled him with pride and nostalgia. It was the Labyrinth at Hawara, a monumental creation that he considered among his finest works. The sight of its enduring form amidst the transformed landscape brought a sense of relief and joy to his heart.

The Labyrinth was more than just a building; it was a testament to the ingenuity and creativity that had defined Thothamak's career. Designed with intricate detail and constructed with precision, the labyrinthine structure was a marvel of engineering and artistry. Its chambers and tunnels were a testament to the architectural prowess of the Atlanteans, a place where knowledge and mystery intertwined.

"I can't believe it has survived," Thothamak said, as he gazed at the Labyrinth. "This is some of my finest work, and I'm so pleased to see it standing strong."

His companions shared in his excitement, eager to explore the structure that had been completed only recently before the cataclysm. The Labyrinth was a place of wonder, a testament to the enduring spirit of creation and the quest for knowledge.

As the ships drew closer to the shore, Thothamak's anticipation grew. The Labyrinth had been designed to withstand the test of time, its walls and corridors constructed from massive stones that spoke to the skill of the artisans who had brought his vision to life. Yet, he couldn't help but wonder if the recent upheavals had left their mark on the structure.

"I hope it hasn't been damaged," Thothamak said, a note of concern in his voice. "The Labyrinth is a symbol of our heritage, a place where the wisdom of the past can guide us into the future."

Once ashore, Thothamak led his companions toward the Labyrinth, the familiar path stirring memories of its construction and the countless hours spent ensuring its perfection. The entrance loomed before them, an imposing gateway that invited exploration and discovery.

Stepping inside, Thothamak was immediately struck by the sense of tranquillity that pervaded the Labyrinth. The air was cool and still, the stone walls echoing with the whispers of ancient knowledge. As they moved through the chambers and tunnels, he marvelled at the craftsmanship that had preserved the structure against the ravages of nature.

The chambers were exactly as he had left them, untouched by the upheaval that had reshaped the world outside. Each room was a testament to the precision and artistry that had gone into its creation, the walls adorned with intricate carvings and symbols that told the stories of their ancestors.

As they explored deeper into the Labyrinth, Thothamak felt a sense of connection to the past, a reminder of the enduring legacy of Atlantis. The structure was more than just a building; it was a repository of knowledge, a place where the wisdom of the ages could be preserved and passed down to future generations.

With newfound determination, Thothamak led his companions deeper into the heart of the Labyrinth, guided by the memories of its intricate design. Each corridor and chamber held a story, a piece of the past carefully preserved in stone. Yet, there was one chamber in particular that called to him—a hidden sanctuary he had designed with a specific purpose in mind.

"This way," Thothamak instructed, his voice echoing softly against the stone walls as he navigated the familiar passages. His companions followed closely, their anticipation growing with each step.

The Labyrinth was a marvel of engineering, each turn and pathway meticulously planned to serve both functional and symbolic purposes. It was a place meant to inspire reflection and discovery, a testament to the enduring spirit of Atlantis. Thothamak had poured his heart into its creation.

At last, they reached their destination—a chamber concealed behind a seemingly ordinary wall. Thothamak approached the wall with a sense of reverence, his fingers tracing the familiar contours of the stone. With a deliberate touch, he activated the hidden mechanism, and the wall shifted, revealing the secret entrance.

"This will be our library," Thothamak announced, stepping into the chamber with a sense of purpose. "Here, we will preserve the ancient knowledge of our people, teaching the ways of the ancients and ensuring that their wisdom is never lost."

His companions followed him inside, their eyes widening at the sight of the chamber. It was a room of considerable size, its walls lined with alcoves and niches designed to hold scrolls and texts. The air was cool and still, a perfect sanctuary for the preservation of knowledge.

The vision for the library was clear in Thothamak's mind. It would be a repository of human achievement, a place where the wisdom of Atlantis could be recorded and shared. The scrolls would contain the teachings of their ancestors, encompassing a vast array of subjects—technologies, astronomy, the links between the planets, and how they influenced life on Earth.

"We will write all of our ancient knowledge on scrolls," Thothamak continued, his voice filled with determination. "The teachings of the ancients, our technologies, our understanding of the cosmos—it will all be preserved here, for the benefit of future generations."

His companions nodded in agreement, inspired by the vision of a library that would stand as a beacon of learning and discovery. The knowledge contained within these walls would be a testament to the ingenuity and wisdom of their ancestors, a guide to creating a future that honoured the past.

As they began to envision the work ahead, Thothamak felt a deep sense of fulfilment and purpose. The library would be a living testament to the spirit of Atlantis, a place where the pursuit of knowledge and understanding could thrive amidst the challenges of a changed world.

"We have much work to do," Thothamak said, a smile playing on his lips as he surveyed the chamber. "But together, we will ensure that the knowledge of Atlantis endures, lighting the way for those who come after us."

Emerging from the sanctuary of the Labyrinth, Thothamak and his companions were filled with a renewed sense of purpose. They had found a place to preserve their knowledge and begin anew, but their mission was far from complete. The land around them, once teeming with vibrant cities and bustling communities, now lay eerily silent—a testament to the devastation that had swept through the region.

Determined to find others who might have survived the cataclysm, Thothamak led the search through the surrounding area. The land was vast and changed, the familiar landscapes reshaped by the surge of water that had swept through, destroying everything in its path.

"We must find any survivors," Thothamak urged his companions, his voice carrying a sense of urgency and hope. "There are bound to be others who need help, who can join us in rebuilding what has been lost."

As they ventured further from the Labyrinth, they began to encounter a few scattered survivors—shepherds and cattlemen who had been working in the hills and highlands, away from the watercourses that had borne the brunt of the tsunami's force. These individuals, accustomed to the solitude of the pastures and fields, had been spared the worst of the devastation.

The sight of these survivors filled Thothamak with a sense of relief and possibility. Though they were few in number, each person represented a thread of hope, a connection to the life that had once thrived in the region.

"Thank the gods, you're alive," Thothamak said, greeting a weathered shepherd who stood with his flock on a hillside. "We're gathering survivors, pooling our knowledge and resources to rebuild."

The shepherd nodded, his expression a mixture of gratitude and disbelief. "I saw the waters rise," he said, his voice carrying the weight of the experience. "It came so fast, swept everything away. Those of us in the hills were lucky."

The city folk, townspeople, and those who had lived and worked in the lowlands were not as fortunate. The cities and towns, built along the watercourses for their bounty and access, had been obliterated by the tsunami. Workshops, technology colleges, libraries—centres of knowledge and progress—all were gone, submerged beneath the newly risen sea.

The realization was a sombre one, a stark reminder of the fragility of human endeavour in the face of nature's might. Yet, amidst the loss, there was a sense of resilience and determination among those who had survived.

"We will rebuild," Thothamak assured the survivors, his voice filled with resolve. "We have knowledge to share and skills to teach. Together, we can create something new, something that honours the past and embraces the future."

As they continued their search, Thothamak's companions began to gather the survivors, guiding them back to the Labyrinth—a sanctuary where they could regroup and plan for the future. The journey was not easy, but each step brought them closer to the goal of rebuilding a society rooted in the values of Atlantis.

The survivors, though scattered and few, represented the seeds of a new beginning. Their resilience and spirit were a testament to the enduring nature of the human spirit, a reminder that even in the face of great loss, hope and renewal were possible.

As the survivors gathered within the protective embrace of the Labyrinth, Thothamak sought out those who might hold remnants of the lost world—fragments of the technology that had once defined their civilization. His heart was heavy with the knowledge that while he possessed the skills to use these innovations, the means to recreate them were beyond his grasp.

Approaching a survivor who had been a craftsman and trader, Thothamak posed the question that weighed heavily on his mind. "Have any of the technologies survived? Anything that we could use or preserve for the future?"

The craftsman, a man of modest build with eyes that spoke of resilience, shook his head solemnly. "I'm afraid not, Thothamak. All the workshops, the tools, the machines—they were destroyed. When the waters came, they took everything with them."

The words were a bitter confirmation of what Thothamak had feared. The workers and technicians who had held the intricate knowledge of building and maintaining their advanced technologies were gone, their expertise lost to the depths. Without them, the future of these innovations seemed dim, a reminder of the civilization that had once thrived.

"I feel as though I'm filled with skills and abilities that can no longer be used," Thothamak confessed, a sense of frustration and helplessness seeping into his voice. "It's as if we've been thrust back into the shadows, and it will take thousands of years for civilization to reach the point where it's ready for this technology again."

The craftsman nodded in understanding; his expression sympathetic. "But you have something that can't be washed away by the sea—knowledge. You and these survivors are the keepers of that wisdom. It may take time, but the seeds of understanding are planted in each of you."

Thothamak took a deep breath, the craftsman's words offering a glimmer of hope amidst the despair. While the physical manifestations of their technology were lost, the knowledge and principles behind them were not entirely gone. They lived on in the minds of those who had survived, in the teachings and wisdom that could be passed down to future generations.

"We must focus on preserving what we know," Thothamak resolved, his voice gaining strength with each word. "We may not have the means to recreate our technology now, but we can ensure that the knowledge is not lost. We will teach, we will write, and we will build a foundation for the future."

With the urgency of preservation weighing heavily on his mind, Thothamak called all the survivors together within the central chamber of the Labyrinth. The air was filled with a sense of anticipation and hope, a shared understanding that the knowledge they possessed was a precious resource—one that needed to be safeguarded for future generations.

Standing before the gathered crowd, Thothamak addressed them with a voice that carried both authority and earnest appeal. "We find ourselves in a time of great challenge and opportunity. Though much has been lost, our knowledge remains. I can share the ancient methods, technologies, and wisdoms that have been entrusted to me. But to ensure their survival, we must commit them to a medium that will endure."

His gaze swept across the faces of the survivors, searching for those who might possess the skills he sought. "Do we have any scribes among us?" he asked, the importance of the question clear in his tone. "We need individuals who can inscribe this knowledge onto clay tablets. Papyrus sheets, while useful, will not survive the length of time needed between now and when civilization catches up with us."

A murmur spread through the crowd as individuals exchanged glances, considering their own skills and experiences. Slowly, a few individuals stepped forward.

One of them, a woman with steady hands and a thoughtful demeanour, spoke up. "I have some experience in inscribing clay tablets," she said, her voice steady and sure. "Though I was not a scribe by trade, I assisted in the temples and learned the methods."

Another survivor, a man with a scholarly air, nodded in agreement. "I, too, have some knowledge," he added. "I studied the ancient scripts and can help with the task."

Thothamak's heart swelled with gratitude and hope as he looked upon those who had come forward. Though their numbers were few, their willingness to contribute their skills to the preservation of knowledge was a testament to the resilience and spirit of their community.

"Thank you," Thothamak said, his voice filled with earnest appreciation. "Your skills are invaluable, and together, we will ensure that the wisdom of Atlantis endures."

With the scribes identified, Thothamak began to organize the task ahead. He shared with them the methods and techniques necessary to create durable clay tablets, emphasizing the importance of precision and care in their work. Each tablet would be a vessel for the knowledge that had been passed down through generations—a legacy that would guide future civilizations.

The survivors worked together, gathering materials and setting up a dedicated area within the Labyrinth where the scribes could carry out their work. The process was meticulous, requiring patience and attention to detail. Yet, despite the challenges, there was a sense of purpose and camaraderie that infused their efforts.

As the first tablets began to take shape, Thothamak felt a deep sense of fulfilment. The knowledge of Atlantis—the technologies, the wisdom, the understanding of the cosmos—was being preserved for the future, ensuring that the legacy of their civilization would not be lost to the sands of time.

The task was far from complete, but each inscribed tablet represented a step toward the future—a future where the achievements of the past could inspire and guide those who came after them. Together, Thothamak and the survivors were building a bridge between the past and the future, one clay tablet at a time.

Together, they began to discuss ways to document and preserve the knowledge they carried, to ensure that the legacy of Atlantis would endure. The Labyrinth, with its hidden chambers and sanctuaries, would serve as the repository of this wisdom—a library where the teachings of their ancestors could be safeguarded and shared.

As the work of inscribing the clay tablets progressed, Thothamak observed the dedication and precision of the scribes with a sense of pride. However, he soon realized that the task of committing all the knowledge to clay tablets, one at a time, was a monumental endeavour that could take years, if not decades, to complete. The urgency of the situation required a more efficient approach to ensure that the wealth of wisdom they possessed would not be lost to time.

Gathering the scribes and survivors once more, Thothamak shared his concerns and proposed a new plan. "The work you are doing is invaluable, and we will continue to inscribe the most critical knowledge onto clay tablets," he began, his voice steady and thoughtful. "However, we must also consider the constraints of time and resources. To preserve all our wisdom, we need a more efficient method."

He then turned his attention to the fastest scribe among them—a young man whose nimble hands and quick mind had already proven invaluable in the initial stages of their work. "We will use papyrus to document the breadth of our knowledge," Thothamak continued. "You will help us capture this information swiftly, creating a comprehensive record that can be preserved and referenced."

The young scribe nodded, understanding the importance of the task. "I will write as quickly as I can," he promised, determination evident in his eyes. "We will create a detailed account of our knowledge, ensuring that nothing is lost."

With the plan in motion, Thothamak and the other scribes worked together to organize the information they needed to document. The papyrus scrolls, though not as durable as clay tablets, would serve as a temporary repository—a means of capturing the full scope of their wisdom quickly and efficiently.

The process required careful coordination, with Thothamak dictating the essential teachings, technologies, and insights that defined the Atlantean legacy. The young scribe's hand moved swiftly across the papyrus, his movements fluid and precise as he recorded the information.

Once the knowledge was documented on papyrus, the plan was to inscribe it onto clay tablets over time, with different scribes taking responsibility for different sections. This approach would not only expedite the initial documentation but also allow for a more organized and systematic preservation of their legacy.

As the papyrus scrolls began to accumulate, Thothamak felt a sense of relief and hope. The knowledge of Atlantis—their understanding of the cosmos, technologies, and the wisdom of the ancients—was being safeguarded, ensuring that future generations would have access to the insights that had shaped their civilization.

"We are building a bridge to the future," Thothamak reminded the survivors, his voice filled with resolve. "While the papyrus is a temporary measure, it will allow us to preserve our knowledge until we can inscribe it onto more permanent mediums. Together, we are ensuring that the legacy of Atlantis endures."

The survivors worked tirelessly, driven by a shared sense of purpose and responsibility. Each scroll, each tablet, represented a piece of their history—a testament to the resilience and ingenuity of their people.

The Lybrinth at Hawara

The Bearers of Light

Chapter 16

With the foundational work within the Labyrinth set in motion, Thothamak felt the call to expand their mission beyond the confines of Egypt. The devastation wrought by the cataclysm had left a world in need of guidance and renewal, and Thothamak, with his seven sages, was determined to spread the seeds of humanity once more.

Gathering the sages, Thothamak shared his vision—a plan to help those who remained, to teach them to live by the Atlantean laws, and to establish a foundation for agriculture and community. It was a mission of hope and resilience, a journey to slowly rebuild civilization with the wisdom of the past as their guide.

"In my hand, I carry the seven personal Atlantean laws," Thothamak said, holding the clay tablets aloft. "These laws are a blueprint for harmony and progress, a guide to creating a world where knowledge and compassion prevail."

He had taken great care to have seven copies of these laws made, one for each sage. The laws were etched into the clay tablets with precision and reverence, each line a testament to the values that had shaped their civilization.

"These tablets are for you," Thothamak continued, distributing a copy to each sage. "Together, you will journey across the Mediterranean then the world, sharing this knowledge and helping those who remain to live in peace and cooperation."

The sages accepted the tablets with solemn nods, their commitment to the mission evident in their eyes. Each sage was a beacon of wisdom and understanding, ready to carry the teachings of Atlantis to the farthest reaches of the world.

Thothamak stood at the edge of the labyrinth, the rising sun casting long shadows over the remnants of a once-great civilization. The air was heavy with the scent of salt from the nearby sea, mingled with the faint aroma of scorched earth—a reminder of the cataclysm that had torn through. Behind him, the seven sages who had journeyed with him from the heart of the shattered empire stood in silent reverence, their faces marked by both sorrow and determination.

It had been many moons since the cataclysm had struck, a disaster so devastating that it had reduced their once-glorious empire to ruins. The world as they had known it was gone, swallowed by the earth and the sea. But the knowledge of Atlantis—the wisdom of the seven laws of advancement—could not be allowed to perish. It was their sacred duty to carry it forward, to seed the wisdom of their ancestors into the new world that would inevitably rise from the ashes of the old.

Thothamak turned to face the seven sages, his piercing gaze holding each of theirs in turn.

"The time has come," he said, his voice steady but laced with the weight of responsibility. "You have each learned the seven laws. You understand their power, their potential, and their purpose. Now, you must spread them to the farthest corners of the East, to the lands untouched by the destruction that has befallen our home. You must teach them as they were taught to you, ensuring that the legacy of Atlantis survives."

The sages listened intently. Each of them had been chosen for their unique gifts—insight, wisdom, and mastery of various disciplines. They were scholars, engineers, philosophers, and healers, united by their dedication to preserving the essence of Atlantis.

Their mission was clear: to journey eastward, across unfamiliar lands and unknown seas, to reestablish communities and share the knowledge of Atlantis. They would teach the laws of water, thought, metallurgy, and all the other advancements that had defined their civilization. They would guide the survivors of the cataclysm, helping them to rebuild and to thrive.

But as Thothamak spoke, his thoughts wandered westward, to the other seven sages who had departed before them.

"They were brave," Thothamak said, almost to himself. "The seven who went west." He paused, his voice softening. "I hope they are safe. I hope they found refuge in the cave they sought, and that they too are searching for survivors and rebuilding in the Americas. The journey west was perilous, but they carried with them the same knowledge and the same hope that we carry now. They are our brothers and sisters, and their success is as vital as our own."

The sages nodded silently; their hearts heavy with the memory of their companions. The fourteen of them had been a family, bound together by their shared mission and the bonds of friendship forged in the final days of Atlantis. The decision to split into two groups—one heading east, the other west—had not been made lightly. But it had been necessary. The cataclysm had scattered the survivors across the globe, and the knowledge of Atlantis needed to reach as many people as possible.

The seven who had gone west had chosen the Americas as their destination. They had spoken of vast, fertile lands, of mountains that touched the sky and rivers that stretched endlessly to the horizon. They had hoped to find survivors there, to establish a stronghold where the wisdom of Atlantis could take root and flourish.

But the journey had been fraught with danger. The seas were no longer predictable, their once-familiar currents disrupted by the upheaval of the earth. The western sages had sought refuge in a cave, a place of safety where they could regroup and plan their next steps. Thothamak could only hope that they had survived, that they were even now spreading the laws and rebuilding amidst the ruins.

Thothamak's voice grew firm as he addressed the seven before him once more. "Remember, the laws are not just lessons—they are lifelines. They are the foundation of civilization, the pillars upon which a better future can be built. But they are also powerful, and with power comes responsibility. Teach them wisely. Do not allow them to be twisted or misused. If the knowledge of Atlantis is to endure, it must be carried with integrity and purpose."

The sages bowed their heads in acknowledgment. They understood the gravity of their task. The laws of Atlantis were the most valuable inheritance of their civilization—a legacy that could either uplift humanity or, in the wrong hands, bring even greater destruction.

As the first light of dawn bathed the Labyrinth in gold, the seven sages prepared to depart. Each carried a small bundle of scrolls, tablets, and artifacts—fragments of Atlantis's wisdom carefully preserved for the journey. They embraced Thothamak in turn, their farewells heavy with emotion.

"You have been our guide, our teacher," said Anara, the youngest of the sages. "We will honour your teachings and carry them forward, no matter what we face."

Thothamak placed a hand on her shoulder, his expression both proud and sombre. "Go with courage, Anara. Go with wisdom, all of you. And remember, we are never truly apart. The laws connect us, as do our thoughts and our purpose. Wherever you go, you carry the heart of Atlantis with you."

With that, the seven sages turned and began their journey eastward, their silhouettes growing smaller with each step until they vanished into the horizon.

As Thothamak watched them disappear, he turned his gaze westward. He closed his eyes and whispered a silent prayer for the seven who had gone before, the sages who had ventured into the unknown to save what could be saved.

"May you find shelter, my friends. May you find survivors. And may the wisdom of Atlantis guide you, as it guides us all."

He lingered there for a moment longer, feeling the weight of his responsibilities and the fragility of their mission. The fate of Atlantis's legacy now rested in the hands of fourteen sages, scattered across the globe. But Thothamak held onto hope—hope that they would succeed, and that one day, the wisdom of Atlantis would shine brightly once more, a beacon for all humanity.

As the sages embarked on their journey, Thothamak turned his thoughts to a personal mission—one that had been on his mind since the cataclysm had altered the world. He intended to return to Göbekli Tepe, the last great work he had undertaken before the comet's approach had forced him to leave.

Göbekli Tepe had been a monumental project, its construction a testament to the architectural and spiritual vision that had defined Thothamak's work. Before departing, he had left strict instructions for the site—a temporary burial of the entire structure to preserve it from the impending cataclysm.

"I will return to Göbekli Tepe," Thothamak announced, his voice filled with determination. "When I left, the work had been completed, and I ordered it to be buried for safekeeping. I must see what has become of it."

The decision resonated with a sense of duty and fulfilment. Göbekli Tepe represented a connection to the past and a promise for the future—a place where the teachings of Atlantis could be enshrined and shared with the world.

Thothamak prepared for his journey to Göbekli Tepe. The Mediterranean beckoned, as he and his companions set sail, Thothamak felt a sense of purpose and renewal. The journey was a continuation of their mission—a promise to honour the legacy of Atlantis and to nurture the seeds of civilization.

The waters of the Mediterranean were calm, the horizon stretching endlessly before them as they navigated the unfamiliar routes. Each destination held the promise of new beginnings, a chance to rebuild and restore the threads of humanity that had been severed by the cataclysm.

As they sailed, Thothamak reflected on the journey ahead. The challenge was immense, but so too was the potential for renewal. The teachings of Atlantis, preserved on the clay tablets and carried in their hearts, would guide them as they worked to create a world rooted in peace, knowledge, and hope.

The journey from the Nile to Asia Minor was one of reflection and anticipation for Thothamak. The seas, now higher than they had ever been and still rising, presented a new landscape, one where familiar landmarks were submerged beneath the waters. Yet, guided by instinct and memory, Thothamak navigated the changed waters with determination, his destination clear in his mind.

As the ship neared the shores of Asia Minor, Thothamak felt a surge of emotions. Göbekli Tepe, the site of his last great work before the cataclysm, loomed on the horizon—a place of significance, steeped in the history of their civilization. He had left it partially filled in, a temporary measure to shield it from the impending destruction. Now, he returned with a new purpose, a mission that had crystallized in the wake of their journey.

Stepping onto the land, Thothamak was filled with a sense of familiarity and reverence. Göbekli Tepe stood as he had left it, its ancient stones a testament to the architectural and spiritual vision that had defined his work. The site was a place of power and mystery, a reminder of the past and a promise for the future.

With careful precision, Thothamak and his companions began to excavate a particular area he had constructed—a chamber with a secret door, known only to him. It had been left empty, a blank canvas awaiting the story that was now ready to be told.

As they cleared the chamber, Thothamak's mind turned to the events that had changed the world—the cataclysm that had reshaped the seas and lands, altering the course of history. It was a story that needed to be preserved, a lesson for future generations to learn from and understand.

"This is where we will tell the story of the cataclysm," Thothamak declared, his voice resonating with purpose. "These stones will bear witness to the events that have transpired, a chronicle for those who come after us."

With the chamber prepared, Thothamak began the meticulous work of carving the story into the stones. Each stroke of the chisel was deliberate and precise, the narrative unfolding in symbols and images that captured the essence of the events. The devastation of the tsunami, the rise of the seas, the loss of megafauna and resilience of humanity—all were etched into the stone, a testament to the enduring spirit of their people.

But the story was not only one of destruction; it was also a tale of hope and renewal. Alongside the chronicle of the cataclysm, Thothamak carved a guide—a map that would lead seekers to the Labyrinth in Egypt. There, they would find the secrets of Atlantis, preserved for those who were ready to embrace its wisdom.

"This guide will lead them to the Labyrinth," Thothamak explained to his companions. "It is there that the knowledge of Atlantis is enshrined, awaiting those who are prepared to learn and build a new future."

The work was arduous, yet Thothamak was driven by a sense of duty and fulfilment. The stones of Göbekli Tepe would serve as a bridge between the past and the future, a repository of knowledge and a beacon of hope.

As the final carvings were completed, Thothamak stepped back to survey the chamber. The story of the cataclysm, the guide to the Labyrinth and the seven Atlantean Laws, the enduring spirit of Atlantis were all immortalized in stone—a legacy for the generations to come.

With the chamber sealed, Thothamak felt a sense of completion. Göbekli Tepe would now stand as a testament to the resilience and wisdom of their civilization—a place where the lessons of the past could guide the future.

Thothamak Saying Goodbye To The Seven Sages

The Seven Personal Laws

Chapter 17

Thothamak had completed the carvings within the chamber at Göbekli Tepe, he felt an unwavering commitment to ensure that the wisdom of Atlantis would endure in more ways than one. Alongside the chronicle of the cataclysm and the guide to the Labyrinth, he had carved a tablet inscribed with the seven personal laws of Atlantis—principles that had guided their civilization and would serve as a foundation for the future.

The laws were carved with precision and care, each one a beacon of guidance and inspiration. They reflected the core values of Atlantis, a testament to the civilization's pursuit of knowledge, self-discovery, and the betterment of humanity.

Law 1: Discover and Enhance Your Natural Abilities

"You are born with natural abilities. It is your duty during your time on this Earth to find out what they are, enhance them to your maximum capacity, then teach those who have similar abilities to you and encourage them to find their path."

Thothamak knew that self-discovery and personal growth were essential to building a meaningful life. This law encouraged individuals to explore their unique talents and share them with others, fostering a community of learning and support.

Law 2: Unlock Your True Potential

"All you need to live a meaningful and fulfilled life is already within you. Your mind is the key to unlocking your true potential. You have a connection to all your past ancestors; their skills and abilities flow within you. Master your mindset through study and implementation."

This law emphasized the power of the mind and the importance of introspection. By tapping into the wisdom of their ancestors and mastering their mindset, individuals could unlock their full potential and live fulfilling lives.

Law 3: Cultivate a Positive Circle of Influence

"You will have a circle of influence throughout your life—people you will meet from childhood through to old age. Make sure you are a positive influence on all these people, from family to friends and acquaintances. This is your circle of influence."

Thothamak understood the impact of interpersonal relationships and the importance of being a positive force in the lives of others. This law encouraged individuals to nurture their connections and inspire those around them.

Law 4: Evolve and Improve

"Humans have been evolving for millennia, one generation improving on the next. Make the most of your time here, developing yourself into the best version of yourself so you leave the world slightly better than when you arrived."

This law reminded individuals of their responsibility to evolve and improve, both personally and collectively. By striving for self-betterment, they could contribute to the ongoing progress of humanity.

Law 5: Practice Gratitude

"Be grateful for the life you have. Many don't get past childhood; others suffer abuse or war. Many people would be grateful for the life you currently have. Be grateful you have already won life's lottery by being born."

Gratitude was an essential component of a fulfilling life. This law encouraged individuals to appreciate their circumstances and recognize the privilege of existence, fostering a sense of contentment and compassion.

Law 6: Embrace Self-Responsibility

"Your life is a reflection of your choices and actions. Take ownership of your circumstances. Do not blame or complain about them. You alone have the power to change them. Decide how you want your life to be and improve yourself until you create the version of you that will have the life you desire."

This law encapsulated the essence of empowerment and personal accountability. In Atlantis, self-responsibility was seen as the foundation of personal growth and societal progress. By taking ownership of their lives, Atlanteans were encouraged to actively shape their destinies, transforming challenges into opportunities for growth.

Thothamak understood the profound impact of this law. It was a call to action, urging individuals to look inward and recognize that they held the power to change their reality. By embracing self-responsibility, Atlanteans could cultivate resilience and determination, forging a path toward self-improvement and fulfilment.

Law 7: Foster Unity and Collective Harmony

"Remember that you are part of a greater whole. Your actions affect not only yourself but also those around you. Strive for harmony in your relationships and with nature. When you foster unity, you contribute to a more balanced and peaceful world."

The final law was a testament to the interconnectedness of all things. In Atlantis, the concept of unity extended beyond human relationships to encompass the natural world. This law emphasized the importance of living in harmony, recognizing that individual actions had far-reaching consequences.

Thothamak knew that the strength of Atlantis lay in its sense of community and collective consciousness. By fostering unity, Atlanteans could create a society that thrived on cooperation and mutual respect. This law served as a reminder that the well-being of one was intrinsically linked to the well-being of all.

As he etched the final strokes, Thothamak felt a sense of completion. The Seven Laws of Atlantis were now immortalized in the stones of Göbekli Tepe—a beacon of wisdom and hope for future generations.

The laws were more than just words; they were the embodiment of a civilization's ideals and aspirations. They held the promise of renewal and the potential to guide humanity toward a brighter future.

But his mission was far from over. The legacy of Atlantis, begun by Poseidon himself, needed to be further safeguarded and spread across the world.

Thothamak knew that the key to humanity's continued advancement lay not only in these personal laws but also in the Seven Laws of Advancement, which were intricately stored within the Labyrinth—a marvel of Atlantean engineering and philosophy. Together, these two sets of laws would provide a comprehensive guide for personal growth and societal progress, ensuring that the legacy of Atlantis would endure for millennia.

Thothamak chose to carry the wisdom of the Atlantean tablets with him, becoming a living emissary of the ancient civilization's ideals. He understood that the world was vast and diverse, with countless cultures and societies each at different stages of development. Since the cataclysm had wiped the slate clean. His purpose was now clear: to journey across the lands, sharing the knowledge and principles that could guide humanity towards a harmonious and enlightened future.

Throughout his journey, Thothamak remained a humble seeker of knowledge, learning as much as he taught. He understood that the legacy of Atlantis was not a static set of rules, but a dynamic and evolving philosophy that could adapt to the unique needs and aspirations of each culture.

As the years passed, Thothamak became a legendary figure, known as the Keeper of Wisdom, a guardian of ancient truths who walked among the people, offering guidance and inspiration. His presence was a reminder that the legacy of Atlantis was alive and thriving, a beacon of hope for a world in need of renewal.

Eventually, Thothamak felt the pull of the tablets, a sense that the time to return them to their sacred places had come. He knew that humanity was on the cusp of great transformation, and that the wisdom of the tablets would one day be rediscovered by those ready to embrace their teachings.

With reverence and care, Thothamak journeyed back to Göbekli Tepe and the Labyrinth. There, he sealed the tablets within their respective places, leaving behind a legacy that would endure through the ages. The knowledge of Atlantis was now intertwined with the fabric of human history, waiting for the moment when it would once again illuminate the path forward.

His life's work complete, he continued to wander, a custodian of wisdom and a bridge between the past and the future. He carried with him the hope that humanity would one day realize the full potential of the Atlantean teachings, forging a world where wisdom and community stood at the heart of civilization, not war and conquest.

Throughout his journey, he had carried with him a persistent longing—a desire to return to the shores of his lost homeland, Atlantis. The destruction of the fabled island had not only shattered a great civilization but had also left a deep void in his heart. Driven by a yearning to reconnect with his roots, Thothamak endeavoured on numerous occasions to sail back to the remnants of Atlantis, navigating through what was once the Pillars of Hercules.

The journey was fraught with challenges, as the sea path westward was now obscured by an immense expanse of mud and debris. The cataclysm that had swallowed Atlantis had forever altered the landscape and the ocean, creating an impassable barrier that thwarted any attempt to venture further into the Atlantic. This disheartening sight led to the region being called the "End of the Known World," a symbolic boundary that marked the limits of human exploration and understanding in the years following the catastrophe.

Thothamak's repeated attempts to breach this barrier were met with failure, yet they served as poignant reminders of the fragility of human endeavour and the power of nature's forces. He realized that

Atlantis, as it once was, could never be reclaimed, but its spirit and teachings could live on through the wisdom he shared with others.

In the aftermath of Atlantis' fall, humanity had been set back thousands of years. The collapse of the great civilization had plunged the world into an age where survival became the primary focus. The arts, philosophy, and astrology, once thriving in the Atlantean golden age, were now practiced by only a handful of individuals scattered across distant lands. Without the unifying influence of Atlantis, these disciplines were kept alive by solitary seekers and small communities who held onto the flickering torch of knowledge.

The vast distances between these isolated groups meant that conflict and war were rare occurrences. Humanity, reduced in numbers and spread thin across the globe, found itself in a period of relative peace. The absence of large-scale conflict allowed for the slow but steady rebuilding of societies, where the focus was on fostering harmony with nature and cultivating a deeper understanding of the world around them.

Thothamak observed these changes with a mixture of hope and melancholy. He saw the resilience of the human spirit in the face of adversity, yet he also mourned the loss of the vibrant intellectual and cultural exchange that had once defined Atlantis. He knew that the legacy of his homeland could not be fully realized until humanity once again reached a state of flourishing, where the pursuit of knowledge and the celebration of creativity could thrive.

Eventually, as humanity's numbers increased and societies grew more complex, the whispers of conflict began to stir once more.

Thothamak understood that this was an inevitable part of the human journey, but he remained steadfast in his belief that the teachings of Atlantis could guide humanity to find balance and harmony amidst the challenges.

He thought of the cyclical nature of history, how civilizations rose and fell, each leaving behind fragments of their knowledge for the next to discover and build upon. He wondered if, when the time came, humanity would have evolved sufficiently to grasp the depth of these laws and use them wisely for the benefit of the future. Would they recognize the significance of what lay beneath the surface, or would the tablets be lost forever, buried by the sands of time and forgotten?

His heart was filled with hope. He believed in the resilience of the human spirit, in the innate curiosity and drive to seek truth and understanding. He had witnessed it in the faces of those he had met on his journeys, in the spark of wonder that flickered in their eyes as they listened to the stories of Atlantis. He knew that, eventually, someone would come who was ready to accept this legacy, to unlock its secrets and share them with the world.

As he walked away from Göbekli Tepe, Thothamak felt a profound sense of peace. He had done all he could to preserve the essence of Atlantis, entrusting its wisdom to the future. The rest was up to the unfolding of time and the choices of those yet to come. He imagined future generations standing where he now stood, feeling the same earth beneath their feet, and he hoped they would be guided by the same desire for growth and enlightenment.

The Seven Atlantean Laws Tablet

The Bridge Between

Chapter 18

Twelve millennia had passed since Thothamak sealed the wisdom of Atlantis within the hidden chamber of Göbekli Tepe. Over the centuries, the world had changed in unimaginable ways, civilizations had risen and fallen, and humanity had ventured beyond the stars. Yet, the core of human curiosity and the quest for knowledge remained unchanged. Now, at the threshold of a new era, Elena found herself standing at the very spot where Thothamak once stood.

Her hands trembled with anticipation as she pushed open the secret door, a barrier untouched by human hands for 12,000 years.

As the door slowly creaked open, a shaft of sunlight pierced the darkness, illuminating the chamber for the first time in millennia. Specks of dust danced in the air, and the ancient stones seemed to breathe in the light, awakening from their long slumber. Elena stepped inside, her footsteps echoing softly in the sacred space.

Her eyes adjusted to the dim light, and she found herself drawn to the far wall, where a stone tablet stood, its presence commanding the room. The light seemed to focus on it, casting a warm glow that highlighted the intricate carvings etched into its surface. As she approached, the words became clear, their message resonating with an otherworldly clarity:

"I, Thothamak, leave you these 7 Personal Laws of Atlantis. Use them well and share this knowledge."

Elena's heart quickened as she traced the ancient script with her fingers, feeling the grooves and edges carved by a hand long gone. The weight of history and the significance of the moment enveloped her, and she realized that she was standing at the intersection of past and future, a bridge between ancient wisdom and modern understanding.

The seven laws, inscribed with care and intention, spoke to her of self-discovery, personal growth, and the interconnectedness of all things. They were a roadmap for human potential, a guide to living a life of purpose and harmony. Elena understood the responsibility that came with this discovery—the duty to share these teachings with the world and ensure that the legacy of Atlantis would inspire a new generation.

As she stood in the chamber, Elena felt a heartfelt connection to Thothamak, the guardian of these truths. She imagined him in this very spot, pondering the future and placing his trust in the hands of those who would follow. His message had transcended time, reaching across the ages to find a kindred spirit ready to embrace the wisdom he had preserved.

Standing at the precipice of history, Elena felt the weight of her discovery overloading her. The chamber at Göbekli Tepe had revealed the unimaginable proof of Atlantis, a civilization long relegated to myth and legend. The implications of such a find were staggering, a seismic shift in the understanding of human history and civilization's origins.

Yet, as the enormity of the moment settled in, Elena was pulled in two directions. Her heart was torn between the duty to share this monumental discovery with the world and the personal journey that awaited her in Egypt.

As her fingers brushed the intricate carvings on the tablet, her gaze fell upon an inscription she hadn't noticed before. It was faint, almost hidden in the edges of the stone, as though it had been deliberately placed for someone who was meant to find it. The words were not just a map but a message—a guide. Her breath caught as she deciphered them with careful precision: "The Labyrinth awaits. Seek the truth beneath the sands of Khem."

Khem. The ancient name for Egypt. A shiver ran down Elena's spine as she whispered the word aloud, the syllables tasting foreign yet familiar on her tongue. The Labyrinth. Thothamak's guide to the Labyrinth. Could this be the same labyrinth her father had spoken of so often, the one he had spent years searching for in vain? The place he had believed held the key to understanding Atlantis and the mysteries of its downfall?

Her mind raced back to the countless nights she had spent poring over her father's journals. He had been obsessed with the idea of a labyrinth buried beneath the Egyptian sands—a place where he believed the ancients had hidden their greatest secrets. According to his theories, the labyrinth wasn't just a myth or a metaphor; it was a vast underground complex, a repository of knowledge and relics left behind by a civilization far older than the Egypt of the Pharaohs. Her father had spent his life chasing the whispers of its existence, convinced that it held the final link between Atlantis and the ancient world.

The realization hit her like a tidal wave. Could it be that Thothamak, the Atlantean sage, and her father had been chasing the same truth across the gulf of time? Were both their spirits guiding her now, drawing her toward this enigmatic labyrinth to unveil what Atlantis was truly about?

Elena's pulse quickened as she pieced it together. The tablet she held, the wisdom of the seven laws, the references to Thothamak—everything seemed to point to Egypt. It was as if the past and the present were converging, and she was standing at the crossroads of a destiny far larger than herself.

Her father had once written in his journal: "The labyrinth is the key. It is not just a place—it is a story, a gateway to our origins, a bridge between the lost and the found." Elena had dismissed it as poetic musings at the time, but now, standing in the presence of this ancient artifact, she wondered if he had been right all along. The labyrinth wasn't just a myth. It was real. And it was waiting for her.

Elena sat down on the cold stone floor, her mind racing. The Labyrinth of Egypt had been the subject of countless myths and legends. Some said it was a maze of endless chambers filled with treasures and traps, built to guard the secrets of the gods. Others believed it was a library, a repository of ancient knowledge left behind by a civilization that had vanished without a trace. But what if it was something more? What if it was the final resting place of Atlantis's greatest wisdom, hidden away by the sages who had fled the cataclysm?

She thought of Thothamak, was he the leader of the seven sages, she had heard about in countless origin stories of different countries? had he carved these tablets to ensure that its legacy would endure even in the face of destruction. Could this labyrinth have been part of that plan? Was it possible that Thothamak himself had journeyed to Egypt, leaving behind a guide for those who would one day seek the truth?

Elena's mind swirled with questions. Why Egypt? What was it about this land that had drawn both Thothamak and her father across the millennia? Was it the power of its ancient civilization, with its towering pyramids and enigmatic gods? Or was it something deeper, something older—a connection to Atlantis itself?

She thought of her father's words, written in the margins of one of his journals: "The labyrinth is not just a place of the past. It is a place of becoming. To find it is to understand where we came from—and where we are going."

This was no coincidence. She was meant to find the labyrinth. She was meant to follow the path that had been laid out before her by both the sage of Atlantis and her own father. It was as if their spirits were working in tandem, guiding her toward a truth that had been buried for thousands of years.

Elena stood, clutching the tablet tightly to her chest. She knew what she had to do. The labyrinth was calling her, and she would answer. She would go to Egypt, to the land of Khem, and she would follow the guide left by Thothamak. There, beneath the shifting sands, she would uncover the secrets of the labyrinth—the story of Atlantis, and perhaps the story of humanity itself.

But as she prepared for the journey ahead, a flicker of doubt crept into her mind. What if the labyrinth was never meant to be found? What if its secrets were hidden for a reason, meant to be protected from the prying eyes of a world not yet ready to understand them?

Elena shook the thought away. If there was one thing she had learned from her father, it was that the pursuit of truth was never without risk. And if there was one thing, she had learned from Thothamak, it was that the wisdom of the past was the key to building a better future.

With a deep breath, she stepped out of the ruins and into the light of a new day. The journey to Egypt awaited, and with it, the answers she had spent her entire life searching for.

The labyrinth was waiting. And so was the truth of Atlantis. Her father, a man whose life had been dedicated to unravelling the mysteries of the past, had passed away, leaving behind a legacy of his own. She had promised herself she would pay her final respects and see if he had left any clues to the ancient door of the Labyrinth and what secrets it might hold.

The decision weighed heavily on her. To announce the discovery of Atlantis would ignite a global frenzy, attracting scholars, explorers, and adventurers of all kinds. It would thrust Elena into the spotlight, a position she had never sought. Yet, she knew the world deserved to know the truth, to be inspired by the teachings of Atlantis that could guide humanity toward a brighter future.

On the other hand, Egypt beckoned with its own mysteries. Her father's journals hinted at discoveries that could be just as transformative, particularly concerning the Labyrinth—a place shrouded in myth, rumoured to contain knowledge that could change the course of history. Elena felt a deep connection to her father's work, knowing that his love for ancient wisdom had shaped her own path.

As she contemplated her next move, Elena realized that these two paths were not mutually exclusive. Both were integral to the unfolding of her journey, and perhaps, they were threads of the same tapestry, woven together by the legacy of Atlantis and her father's indomitable spirit.

Her decision made; Elena resolved to honour both responsibilities. She would secure the chamber at Göbekli Tepe, ensuring that its secrets remained protected until the time was right to share them. She would then travel to Egypt, guided by her father's notes and her own intuition, to uncover what he had found and see if it connected to the Atlantean legacy.

Before leaving Göbekli Tepe, Elena took meticulous notes, documenting the chamber and its contents with precision. She knew that one day, she would return and reveal the discovery, ensuring that the wisdom of Atlantis would illuminate the path for future generations.

With her preparations complete, Elena set her sights on Egypt, her heart filled with both anticipation and trepidation, she was driven by a sense of destiny, knowing that her father's work and the secrets of the Labyrinth were crucial pieces in the puzzle of Atlantis.

Elena Feeling Thothamak And Her Fathers Spirits Guiding Her

The Legacy Discovered

Chapter 20

The journey to Egypt had been fraught with emotion and anticipation. As Elena navigated the bustling streets of Cairo, her heart was laden with the knowledge of what awaited her. Her father, a man who had been her mentor and inspiration, lay in the morgue, a stark reminder of the fragility of life and the relentless passage of time.

Entering the sterile, cold confines of the morgue, she felt a chill that had nothing to do with the temperature. It was the chill of finality, the realization that she would never again hear her father's voice or see his encouraging smile. Her heart ached with the weight of unspoken words and shared dreams unfulfilled.

As she approached the table where his body lay, she was gripped by an extreme sense of loss. Her father, a brilliant archaeologist who had devoted his life to uncovering the secrets of the past, had so much more to offer the world. His passion for discovery and his unwavering belief in the potential of ancient wisdom had been the guiding stars of his existence.

Seeing him there, lifeless and still, Elena's composure broke, and she was overwhelmed by a wave of grief. Tears streamed down her face as she reached out to touch his hand, the hand that had unearthed countless relics and penned volumes of insights into the mysteries of history. She whispered a silent goodbye, her heart heavy with sorrow and regret.

Yet, amidst the tears, a resolve began to take shape. Elena knew that her father would not have wanted her to be consumed by grief. He had always encouraged her to pursue her passions and to carry forward the torch of knowledge and discovery. In that moment, she made a promise to herself and to him: she would continue his work, honouring his legacy by delving into the mysteries he had left behind.

She had so much to tell him about her findings at Göbekli Tepe, about the hidden chamber and the secrets it held. She longed to share the excitement of her discovery and to hear his thoughts on the implications of Atlantis's existence. And there was the Labyrinth, the enigmatic structure her father had been so fascinated by.

Gathering her strength, Elena was determined to carry on. She would explore the Labyrinth, following the clues her father had left, and uncover the secrets he had been so close to revealing. She would ensure that his work was not in vain, that his contributions to the understanding of ancient civilizations would be honoured and celebrated.

She kissed his forehead one last time, reliving all the times he had kissed hers, and her tears caught the side of his face and ran down his cheek, as if he too were saying goodbye for the last time.

Leaving the morgue, Elena felt a sense of determination mingling with her grief. Her father had passed the baton to her, entrusting her with the continuation of his life's mission. She was ready to embrace the challenge, driven by the knowledge that she was not alone. Her father's spirit, along with the legacy of Thothamak and Atlantis, would guide her.

Elena left the morgue and went straight to her father's apartment, a place filled with memories and echoes of a life dedicated to discovery. The familiar scent of old books and the sight of artifacts from various digs around the world enveloped her in a comforting embrace. Yet, as she moved through the rooms, her heart ached with the absence of the man who had been her guiding light.

The old photographs scattered throughout the apartment were bittersweet reminders of the bond they shared. Images of her as a child, perched on her father's knee, listening intently as he spun tales of ancient worlds and hidden treasures. Pictures from their first dig together, both covered in dust and beaming with the thrill of discovery. Each photo was a testament to their shared journey, now tinged with the pain of loss.

As she wandered through the apartment, Elena's eyes fell upon her father's collection of diaries, meticulously kept over the years. These volumes were the chronicles of his life, each one filled with insights, observations, and the minutiae of daily life on archaeological digs. The diaries were a window into his mind, a record of his thoughts and dreams.

With a sense of reverence, Elena began to leaf through the pages, feeling the weight of history in every entry. It was a journey through time, each page bringing her closer to her father and the work that had defined him. As she read, she could almost hear his voice, the cadence of his words a familiar comfort.

Tears were streaming down her face, each drop carrying the weight of missed opportunities and unshared discoveries. Her trembling fingers traced the edges of the weathered pages, feeling the slight indentations where his pen had pressed into the paper. She so wanted to share her discovery and his discovery one last time - to see his eyes light up with that familiar spark of enthusiasm, to hear his voice rise with excitement as he connected the historical dots.

When she reached the final diary, her heart quickened. This was the one he had been writing in at the time of his death. The last entry was penned just before he had planned to call her. Her eyes scanned the page, absorbing his words, each one a poignant reminder of his unwavering dedication to his work. The ink still looked fresh, as if he had just lifted his pen from the paper, his presence somehow lingering in every carefully formed letter.

"I've found it," he had written with palpable excitement. "A secret door inside the Labyrinth. I managed to creep inside. There were many jars filled with scrolls and clay tablets with lists on them—possibly ancient laws, but I couldn't see clearly. I need Elena here. I'll call her later; she will absolutely love this."

As she read the words, Elena felt a surge of emotion, a mixture of pride and sorrow. Her fingers ghosted over his handwriting, touching the last words he'd ever write. The phrase "she will absolutely love this" pierced her heart like an arrow - he had known her so well, understood exactly what would fascinate her. Now these words were all that remained of their shared passion, their mutual quest for understanding the ancient world. The diary trembled in her hands as fresh tears fell, creating small dark circles on the aged paper, her present grief mixing with his past joy in a bitter testament to what could have been.

Her father had been on the brink of a monumental discovery, one that could potentially unlock the secrets of the Labyrinth and reveal insights into ancient civilizations. He had wanted her to be a part of it, to share in the excitement and wonder of the find.

The entry was a message from beyond urging her to continue the work they had begun together. The Labyrinth held answers, and it was up to her to uncover them. Her father had believed in her abilities, in her passion for discovery, and now it was her turn to honour that belief by stepping into the unknown.

Elena knew what she had to do. She would go to the Labyrinth, guided by her father's notes and Thothamak's directions. The promise of scrolls and tablets, possibly containing laws akin to those she had found at Göbekli Tepe, was too significant to ignore. The task was daunting, but she was ready to embrace it, fuelled by the knowledge that her father would be with her in spirit.

Armed with her father's notes and her own determination, Elena set out to retrace the steps he had taken within the enigmatic Labyrinth. Her heart was a mix of anticipation and solemnity as she approached the ancient structure, a place steeped in mystery and the whispers of forgotten secrets. The Labyrinth loomed before her; its entrance shadowed by the passage of countless centuries.

Following the instructions detailed in her father's meticulous notes, Elena navigated the winding corridors of the Labyrinth. The air was thick with the scent of antiquity, a blend of dust and history that seemed to cling to her skin.

The path was dimly lit, the only illumination coming from the intermittent beams of sunlight that filtered through cracks in the stone. The sand underfoot shifted with every movement, adding to the sense of being enveloped in a tomb—a resting place for ancient knowledge waiting to be unearthed.

Elena's heart raced as she approached the location her father had described in his notes. She crawled along the narrow passageway, her hands brushing against the cool, rough surface of the stone walls. The journey was arduous, but her resolve never wavered. She was driven by the promise of discovery and the desire to honour her father's legacy.

Finally, she reached the spot where her father had marked the presence of the secret door. It was buried up to the top in sand, a nearly imperceptible seam in the stone that seemed to defy detection. Yet, just as her father had noted, the door had cracked, creating a narrow opening just wide enough for her to slide through.

Elena took a deep breath, steeling herself for what lay beyond. She felt a connection to her father, imagining him making this same journey, driven by the same sense of wonder and curiosity. With determination, she began to manoeuvre her way through the opening, feeling the rough edges of the stone against her skin.

As she emerged on the other side, Elena found herself in a chamber that seemed untouched by time. The air was still and cool, carrying with it the faint echo of history. The room was dimly lit by a natural aperture in the ceiling that allowed a single beam of sunlight to illuminate the space, casting an ethereal glow.

Her eyes were immediately drawn to the array of jars and tablets that occupied the chamber, just as her father had described. The jars were ancient, their surfaces etched with intricate designs, while the clay tablets bore inscriptions that hinted at the wisdom they contained. Elena felt a thrill of excitement and reverence as she realized the significance of what she had found.

This was the culmination of her father's work, the secret he had been so close to revealing. The tablets and scrolls could hold the laws and teachings that had been lost to time, potentially offering insights into the civilizations that had once thrived here. Elena knew that these artifacts could change the understanding of history and humanity's place within it.

With careful hands, she began to examine the contents of the chamber, documenting her findings with the precision her father had taught her. Each piece was a fragment of a larger puzzle, a part of human history that she was determined to unravel.

As she worked, Elena felt her father's presence beside her, guiding her actions and inspiring her with the passion that had driven him throughout his life. She knew that this discovery was not just hers, but theirs—a shared triumph that transcended the boundaries of life and death.

In the dim and sacred chamber of the Labyrinth, Elena's eyes locked onto a particular tablet. Its surface, as fresh as if it were carved yesterday, bore an inscription that sent a shiver down her spine. She could scarcely believe what she was seeing, yet the familiar words were unmistakable:

"I, Thothamak, leave you these seven Laws of Atlantean Advancement. Use them well and share this knowledge."

A wave of emotion crashed over Elena, leaving her trembling with disbelief. She had stumbled upon the very heart of Atlantean wisdom, the laws that had once guided a civilization of unparalleled advancement and harmony. Here, in this hidden chamber, lay the tangible proof of Atlantis's existence and its profound contributions to human understanding.

The seven laws of advancement, inscribed by Thothamak and preserved through the ages, were a blueprint for humanity's harmonious progress, a testament to the wisdom of Atlantis and its understanding of the natural world. These laws held the potential to guide civilizations toward enlightenment, offering insights into how the forces of nature could be harnessed for the betterment of all.

The first of these laws focused on one of the most fundamental yet misunderstood forces: sound. The inscription on the ancient tablet was both elegant and profound, its words etched in a flowing script that seemed to hum with a resonance of their own. As Elena read the first law, she felt a sense of awe at the depth of knowledge it conveyed:

Law 1 The power of sound

"Everything is in a condition of vibration. If you match this vibration in harmony, you can speed up repair to any part of the human body. This also works in nature with stone, especially those with a high crystal content. However, if you use the opposing vibration, you will cause damage and illness to the body, as well as to nature. Study this form well—it can advance many areas."

Elena let the words sink in, her mind racing with the implications of this discovery. The Atlanteans had understood sound not just as a phenomenon to be heard, but as a fundamental force that influenced the very fabric of existence. Everything in the universe, from the smallest atom to the grandest mountain, vibrated at its own unique frequency. To understand these vibrations was to hold the key to healing, creation, and destruction.

The Law of Sound, as described, was a dual-edged sword. In harmony, it could be a force of rejuvenation and growth; in discord, it could bring ruin and decay. This duality was a reminder of the responsibility that came with knowledge, a warning to wield such power wisely.

Thothamak's inscription spoke of the body's vibrations and how matching them in harmony could accelerate repair. Elena envisioned the possibilities: sound waves tuned to the specific frequency of damaged organs or tissues, stimulating them to regenerate and heal. It was a concept that resonated with modern theories of resonance and frequency, but here it was described with a clarity and depth that surpassed anything she had encountered before.

In Atlantis, the use of sound for healing had been a cornerstone of their medical practices. Ancient records hinted at chambers designed to amplify specific frequencies, where individuals could immerse themselves in vibrations tailored to their needs. These sound healing chambers, constructed with materials rich in crystalline minerals, created an environment where harmony resonated through every cell of the body.

Elena wondered how this knowledge could revolutionize modern medicine. From repairing broken bones to regenerating damaged organs, the applications seemed limitless. She could almost hear her father's voice, brimming with excitement at the thought of uncovering such a transformative truth.

The inscription also spoke of sound's effect on nature, particularly on stone, with a focus on those containing high levels of crystalline content. The Atlanteans had harnessed this principle in their architecture and engineering, using sound to shape and repair massive stone structures. Vibrations tuned to resonate with the molecular structure of the stone allowed them to move and manipulate even the largest blocks with ease, a technology that modern scientists could scarcely fathom.

Elena recalled stories of ancient monuments, like the pyramids of Egypt or the enigmatic stones of Stonehenge and wondered if their construction had been informed by similar principles. Could the ancients have shared this knowledge, fragments of Atlantean wisdom passed down through the ages? It was a tantalizing possibility that hinted at a deeper connection between humanity's greatest achievements.

Yet, as with all great power, sound carried inherent risks. The inscription warned of the destructive potential of opposing vibrations, capable of causing illness in the body and devastation in nature. Elena shuddered at the thought of such misuse, imagining the catastrophic consequences of sound wielded as a weapon.

In Atlantis, the ethical use of sound had been a matter of great importance. Thothamak had emphasized the need for balance, urging his people to study this force not only for its potential but also for its dangers. The misuse of sound could unravel the harmony that the Atlanteans had worked so hard to achieve, a sobering reminder of the responsibility that came with such knowledge.

As Elena absorbed the teachings of the first law, she felt a strong sense of connection to the people of Atlantis. Their understanding of sound as a force of both creation and destruction reflected their respect for the natural world and their desire to live in harmony with it. This wisdom, preserved through the ages, was a gift to humanity—a chance to rediscover the principles that could guide them toward a brighter future.

Elena's thoughts turned to the present, to the challenges and opportunities that lay ahead. The Law of Sound was more than an ancient teaching; it was a reminder that humanity's advancement depended on its ability to live in balance with the forces of nature. She resolved to share this knowledge with the world, to help others understand the power of sound and its potential to heal, create, and inspire.

Law 2 Harness the sun's power

The second law, etched into the ancient tablet with the same precision and reverence as the first, spoke of the mightiest force known to humanity: the power of the sun. As Elena read the inscription, she could feel the wisdom of Thothamak radiating from the words, his understanding of natural forces as profound as it was timeless:

"The sun is the strongest of powers. It provides life to our planet. Harnessed, it can reduce even the hardest stone to liquid. Follow nature—plants use this amazing resource through photosynthesis to create energy from light. This is a free source of power for everyone; it should be shared to help humanity. When combined with the use of metallurgy, harnessing this power can create either a great tool for constructing magnificent structures or a destructive force capable of annihilating anything in its path."

Elena let the words settle in her mind, the sheer magnitude of their meaning both daunting and inspiring. The Atlanteans had understood the sun not merely as a life-giving celestial body but as the ultimate source of power, a force of creation and destruction that could shape civilizations. The second law was a testament to their genius and their deep respect for the natural world.

The inscription began with the most fundamental truth: the sun was the giver of life. Its warmth and light nurtured the Earth, stimulating the growth of plants and sustaining every living being on the planet. Without the sun, existence itself would be impossible. The Atlanteans had revered this force, recognizing its vital role in the balance of nature.

Elena reflected on the idea of photosynthesis, the process by which plants converted sunlight into energy. It was a perfect system, an elegant combination of biology and physics that had sustained life for millions of years. The Atlanteans had understood this principle deeply, seeing in it a model for humanity to emulate. If plants could transform light into energy, why couldn't humans do the same on a grander scale?

The law emphasized that the sun's power was a "free source of power for everyone." This phrase resonated with Elena—it was a call for equality, a reminder that the sun belonged to all of humanity. In a world where resources were often hoarded and exploited for profit, the Atlanteans had envisioned a future where the sun's energy would be shared freely, lifting civilizations to new heights.

The Atlanteans had not only admired the sun as a source of life—they had learned to harness its immense power in ways that were both practical and revolutionary. The inscription spoke of reducing "the hardest stone to liquid," a concept that stunned Elena. It was a reference to the incredible heat generated by focusing sunlight, a technique that the Atlanteans had mastered with precision.

Elena thought back to stories she had heard of ancient, polished gold semi-spheres used in the defence of a harbour or during a war. Those devices had harnessed the sun's rays to devastating effect, focusing them into a beam of concentrated heat capable of setting ships ablaze. It was both an awe-inspiring and terrifying demonstration of the sun's destructive potential.

But the law also alluded to the constructive applications of solar energy. Combined with metallurgy, the focused power of the sun could melt and shape even the hardest materials, enabling the creation of monumental structures that defied imagination. Elena imagined the Atlanteans using this technology to carve their massive stone temples, their gleaming cities rising like jewels under the sunlit sky. The same force that could destroy could also create wonders, that underscored the need for wisdom in its use.

The second law carried a cautionary note, a reminder of the dangers inherent in wielding such immense power. Harnessing the energy of the sun could "create either a great tool for constructing magnificent structures or a destructive force capable of annihilating anything in its path." The Atlanteans had understood this well, balancing their technological advancements with a sense of responsibility.

Elena felt a pang of unease as she considered the implications. The potential for destruction was not merely theoretical, history was littered with examples of innovations turned to violent ends. Atlantis itself had fallen, its incredible knowledge lost to the ages. The second law was not just a guide; it was a warning. To harness the sun's power responsibly required wisdom, humility, and an unwavering commitment to the greater good.

As Elena studied the second law, she felt a deep connection to the Atlanteans' vision for humanity. The sun, the most abundant and universal source of energy, was meant to be a gift for all, a force to uplift and unify. Yet, the law also acknowledged the fragility of that vision—the temptation to wield power destructively was an ever-present danger.

Modern humanity, Elena realized, was only beginning to unlock the potential of solar energy. Advances in solar panels and renewable energy mirrored the principles described in the law, but there was still so much more to learn. The Atlanteans had gone further, tapping into the sun's power in ways that seemed almost magical. Their knowledge could revolutionize the world, offering solutions to energy crises, environmental degradation, and the inequalities that plagued society.

She resolved to share this law with the world, to reignite the Atlantean dream of a civilization powered by the sun's endless light. It was a legacy of hope and possibility, a chance to honour the wisdom of the past by building a brighter future.

Law 3– The Unlimited Power of Lightning

The third law of advancement, inscribed with the same care and reverence as the first two, described a force of nature that was both astonishing and untamed: the power of lightning. As Elena read the ancient text, she marvelled at the ingenuity of the Atlanteans in understanding and harnessing this seemingly chaotic energy. The inscription was a masterpiece of both science and philosophy, a record of how one of nature's most destructive forces had been transformed into a boundless source of power:

"Long ago, we learned to attract and store the unlimited power of lightning. We harnessed this force, storing it within the crystalline structure of granite. Gold, the great conductor, became our ally, drawing the storms and channelling their energy. From single obelisks to the grand design of the Great Pyramid, we used this immense power to provide wireless electricity to all, spreading energy as freely as the storms themselves. Use this knowledge wisely, for the power of lightning is a gift of the gods, but a dangerous one."

Elena's breath caught as the full implications of the third law dawned on her. The Atlanteans had unlocked the secrets of one of the most unpredictable and destructive forces in nature, turning it into an endless and renewable source of energy. This was no mere theoretical concept—this was applied science, practiced by a civilization that had mastered the elements in ways that modern humanity could barely comprehend.

Thothamak's inscription began with the obelisks, those towering monoliths of solid granite crowned with gold. The Atlanteans had discovered that granite, with its high crystalline content, could hold an electrical charge, much like a natural battery. When lightning struck the gold-tipped obelisks, the energy was drawn into the granite, stored within its crystalline structure, and slowly released over time.

Elena could picture the storms that were said to be more common 12,000 years ago, great tempests that lit up the skies above Atlantis and its surrounding regions. The Atlanteans, rather than fearing the storms, had embraced them as a source of power. They had positioned their obelisks strategically, using them as lightning rods to capture the raw energy of the heavens.

But the brilliance of the Atlanteans didn't stop at capturing lightning—they had also discovered how to use that stored energy. Wireless electricity radiated from the charged granite obelisks, providing power to nearby structures and devices without the need for physical connections. Elena marvelled at the foresight of a civilization that had not only discovered electricity but had also made it accessible to all, a resource for the benefit of their entire society.

The inscription went on to describe a pivotal moment in Atlantean history, when their mastery of lightning inspired an even grander vision. The scattered obelisks, while effective, had their limitations. The Atlanteans dreamed of building a centralized energy source, a structure that could store and distribute power on a massive scale. That dream culminated in the construction of what we now know as the Great Pyramid of Giza.

Elena's heart raced as she read this revelation. The Great Pyramid, often shrouded in mystery and speculation, was described here not as a tomb or monument, but as a colossal power station. The pyramid's design was a masterpiece of engineering, its every element serving a purpose in the storage and transmission of electrical energy.

The pyramid's core was built with massive blocks of granite, each one carefully positioned to act as a reservoir for the energy captured from lightning. The outer casing of limestone served as an insulator, preventing the energy from dissipating and ensuring it could be directed where it was needed. At the very top of the pyramid was a gold capstone, designed to attract lightning during storms and channel the energy down through the structure.

Elena could barely contain her excitement as she imagined the pyramid in its full glory, a beacon of technological achievement. The energy it stored and released would have radiated across vast distances, providing wireless electricity to the surrounding region. The Atlanteans had created a system that was both sustainable and efficient, a testament to their understanding of natural forces and their commitment to using them for the benefit of all.

Yet, as with the first two laws, the third law carried a warning. Lightning was a gift of the gods, but it was also dangerous, its power capable of destruction as well as creation. The Atlanteans had understood this and had taken great care to control and direct the energy they captured. Their use of lightning was a testament to their wisdom, but it also served as a reminder of the thin line between progress and hubris.

Elena thought of the modern world's struggles with energy—its reliance on finite resources, its environmental consequences, and its inequitable distribution. The Atlanteans had solved these problems millennia ago, creating a system that was both renewable and universally accessible. Yet their civilization had fallen, their knowledge lost to time. What mistakes had they made? What lessons could be learned from their rise and fall?

As Elena studied the third law, she felt a strong sense of purpose. The knowledge preserved in these tablets was not just a record of the past—it was a roadmap for the future. The unlimited power of lightning, harnessed and shared responsibly, could revolutionize the way humanity approached energy. It could provide clean, sustainable power to every corner of the globe, lifting billions out of poverty and transforming the way societies functioned.

But more than that, the third law was a reminder of humanity's potential. The Atlanteans had looked to the heavens and seen not chaos, but opportunity. They had dared to dream of harnessing the storms, and in doing so, they had created wonders that still inspired thousands of years later.

The power of lightning, like the sun and sound before it, was a force of nature waiting to be understood and embraced. It was a gift, but also a responsibility—a challenge to use the tools of the natural world not for domination, but for the advancement of all.

The Seven Atlantean Laws Of Advancement Continued

The 4th Law of Advancement – The Power of Electromagnetism

The fourth law of advancement revealed an in-depth understanding of a natural force that shaped the very core of their civilization: electromagnetism. This law described the union of magnetism, which the Atlanteans had revered as a "mystical force," and electricity, combining the two into a powerful and transformative tool. But what set this law apart was the Atlanteans' understanding of the Earth's magnetic field itself, a force that not only sustained life but could be harnessed for energy, navigation, and incredible feats of engineering.

Elena read the inscription, its words resonating with a sense of wonder and discovery:

"Electromagnetism is the union of magnetism and electricity, a force of immense power. Long ago, we unravelled the mystery of magnetism and discovered the Earth's magnetic field—a force that surrounds and sustains our world. This field guides many creatures, such as birds, turtles, and others, in their journeys across the Earth. We learned to use this natural magnetic force not only for navigation but also to create energy. Magnetite, a natural magnet, can both attract and repel. Combined with electricity, it becomes a force capable of incredible feats. Its unique attribute lies in its strength: the heavier the substance, the stronger the force becomes. With this power, colossal stones can be moved with ease, gliding along roads made of the correct stones containing a magnetic current. Use this force wisely—it is one of the Earth's greatest gifts."

The inscription began with a revelation that stunned Elena: The Atlanteans had understood the Earth's magnetic field in ways that modern science was only beginning to explore. They recognized it as a natural and universal force, an invisible field surrounding the planet, protecting it from solar winds and sustaining life. More than that, they had realized its potential as a resource for humanity.

The Earth's magnetic field was not just a passive phenomenon—it was a guide and a source of energy. The Atlanteans had observed how many animals, such as migratory birds and sea turtles, used the magnetic field to navigate vast distances with unerring precision. They had been inspired by these creatures, seeing in their journeys a clue to unlocking the power of magnetism for human use.

By studying the Earth's magnetic field, the Atlanteans had developed tools for navigation, allowing them to explore the world with confidence and accuracy. But their genius extended far beyond navigation. They saw in the magnetic field a source of energy, one that could be harnessed and combined with electricity to create an entirely new force: electromagnetism.

The Atlanteans had long been fascinated by magnetism, a force they described as "mystical" yet deeply rooted in nature. Magnetite, a naturally occurring magnetic mineral, had been their key to understanding this phenomenon. Its ability to attract and repel held the seeds of a great discovery.

Through careful study, the Atlanteans had unravelled the principles of magnetism, understanding how it interacted with other forces, especially electricity. They discovered that by running electrical currents through magnetite, they could amplify its properties, creating an electromagnetic force that was far more powerful than either electricity or magnetism alone.

The inscription described the union of magnetism and electricity as the birth of a new force: electromagnetism. This force had a unique and remarkable attribute: its strength was directly proportional to the weight and magnetic properties of the substances it acted upon. This meant that the heavier and more magnetically receptive an object was, the stronger the electromagnetic force became.

This principle held extraordinary potential. The Atlanteans realized that with the right application of electromagnetism, they could lift and move objects of immense weight—objects that otherwise be immovable.

The Atlanteans had applied this knowledge in ways that seemed almost magical. The inscription described roads made of stones containing magnetic currents, carefully constructed to interact with the electromagnetic force. These magnetic roads became pathways along which even the heaviest stones could be moved with ease.

Elena could almost picture it: the Atlanteans using electromagnetic technology to transport the massive blocks of granite and basalt that formed their great monuments. The stones, infused with a magnetic charge, would glide along the roads as if floating, their immense weight rendered inconsequential by the power of electromagnetism.

This technology explained how the Atlanteans had been able to construct their monumental structures with such precision and efficiency. The Great Pyramid of Giza, the towering obelisks, and the vast temples of Atlantis itself—all these wonders owed their existence, at least in part, to the power of electromagnetism and the Earth's magnetic field.

The inscription also emphasized the Atlanteans' use of electromagnetism for navigation. By aligning their tools with the Earth's magnetic field, they had developed instruments that allowed them to traverse vast distances with accuracy and confidence. This knowledge had enabled them to become master explorers, charting the seas and connecting with distant lands.

But the Atlanteans had not stopped at navigation. They had seen in the Earth's magnetic field a source of energy that could be harnessed for the benefit of all. Their ability to combine this force with electricity had enabled them to create a civilization powered not by finite resources, but by the boundless forces of nature.

As with the other laws, the fourth law carried an implicit warning. The power of electromagnetism was immense, but it was not without risks. The same force that could lift and move colossal stones could also be used to cause destruction.

Elena thought about the modern world's struggles with technology, energy, and ethics. The Atlanteans' mastery of electromagnetism was a lesson in responsibility, a reminder that knowledge and power must be wielded with care. To harness the forces of nature was to take on a great responsibility, one that required wisdom, balance, and a commitment to the greater good.

As she studied the fourth law, she realised. The Atlanteans had achieved feats that seemed impossible, yet their knowledge had been grounded in the natural world. Electromagnetism was not a supernatural force—it was a gift of the Earth, a resource waiting to be understood and utilized.

She imagined the potential applications of this knowledge in the modern world. Electromagnetic technology could revolutionize construction, transportation, and energy. Magnetic roads, electromagnetic propulsion, and navigation tools based on the Earth's magnetic field could transform the way humanity interacted with the planet. Yet, the fourth law also served as a reminder of the importance of balance. Progress must be guided by wisdom, and power must be tempered with responsibility.

The 5th Law of Advancement – The Mastery of Metallurgy

The fifth law of advancement was a celebration of human ingenuity, skill, and the relentless pursuit of knowledge. Carved into the ancient Atlantean tablet, it chronicled the evolution of metallurgy, a field of study that had transformed the way the Atlanteans interacted with the world. Metallurgy was not just a science to them—it was an art, a tradition passed down through generations, refined and perfected until they achieved mastery.

As Elena read the inscription, she could feel the pride and reverence imbued in the words:

"Metallurgy, developed over thousands of years, began with the extraction of metals from natural ores through heat. Over time, we learned to combine metals, creating alloys with unique properties for specific tasks. Our craft, honed through generations, made us master metallurgists. The strongest metal we created was an alloy of tungsten and orichalcum, capable of withstanding over 6,000 degrees Fahrenheit before melting. With this metal, we shaped the Earth, cutting granite with precision and creating earthquake-proof structures. From the ores of meteorites, we forged metals with extraordinary strength, reaching beyond the heavens. This is the legacy of our craft."

The inscription began with the origins of metallurgy, a technology that had emerged from humanity's earliest attempts to tame fire and extract useful materials from the Earth. The Atlanteans had started by observing natural ores—raw minerals embedded in rocks—and experimenting with heat to extract the metals within. This process required both curiosity and ingenuity, as they learned to control fire and develop techniques for smelting.

Elena imagined the early Atlanteans working over roaring furnaces, their faces lit by the glow of molten metal. These pioneers had unlocked the secrets of nature, transforming raw stone into tools and weapons that elevated their civilization. But the Atlanteans hadn't stopped there. They had seen the potential for metals to be more than simple tools—they had envisioned a future where metals would shape the world itself.

The real breakthrough in Atlantean metallurgy came with the discovery of alloying: the process of combining two or more metals to create a new material with enhanced properties. This innovation was a game-changer, allowing the Atlanteans to tailor metals for specific purposes. Some alloys were designed for strength, others for flexibility, and still others for resistance to heat or corrosion.

The inscription spoke of the skill and craftsmanship required to perfect this process. Metallurgy was not merely a technical discipline—it was a form that demanded patience, precision, and a deep understanding of the materials being used. The knowledge of alloying was passed down from generation to generation, each new discovery building on the work of those who had come before.

By the height of their civilization, the Atlanteans had become master metallurgists, capable of creating metals that surpassed anything the world had seen.

The pinnacle of Atlantean metallurgy was the creation of an alloy combining tungsten and orichalcum. Tungsten, known for its incredible melting point and hardness, was an exceptional metal in its own right. Orichalcum, the legendary metal of Atlantis, was equally remarkable, prized for its strength and conductivity. Together, these two metals formed an alloy that was virtually indestructible.

The inscription described this alloy as capable of withstanding temperatures over 6,000 degrees Fahrenheit, far beyond the melting point of most other materials. This property made it invaluable for construction and engineering. Elena was particularly struck by its use in cutting stone.

The Atlanteans had used tools made from this alloy to cut through granite, a material that melted at just over 2,200 degrees Fahrenheit. With their incredible heat resistance, these tools could slice through granite as if it were butter, following the contours of the previous block with precision. The result was a perfect fit between stones, requiring no mortar to hold them together.

Elena imagined the construction of Atlantean monuments, the massive blocks of stone fitting together so seamlessly that even a razor blade couldn't pass between them. These structures were not only beautiful but also earthquake-proof, their interlocking design allowing them to withstand the shifting of the Earth. It was a testament to the Atlanteans' ingenuity and their ability to combine science and art in service of their vision.

The inscription also spoke of metals forged from meteorites, materials that had fallen from the heavens. These extraterrestrial ores were rare and precious, possessing unique properties that made them exceptionally strong. The Atlanteans had recognized their value and incorporated them into their metallurgical practices, creating alloys that pushed the boundaries of what was possible.

Elena was captivated by the idea of the Atlanteans working with materials from beyond the Earth. It was a reminder of their ambition and their ability to see the potential in every resource. To them, the cosmos was not a distant mystery—it was a source of inspiration and discovery.

As with the other laws, the fifth law was not just a description of technology—it was a celebration of the human spirit. The Atlanteans had achieved mastery of metallurgy through generations of dedication and effort, their knowledge growing with each new discovery. They had approached their craft with humility and reverence, understanding that the materials they worked with were gifts of the Earth and the heavens.

Elena thought about the modern world's reliance on metals, from the steel that built skyscrapers to the copper that powered electrical grids. The Atlanteans' legacy was alive in every tool, every machine, and every structure. Yet, their approach to metallurgy was different. They had seen it not as an industry, but as an art—a way of connecting with the natural world and shaping it in harmony with their vision.

The fifth law, like the others, carried an implicit warning. Mastery of metallurgy was a great achievement, but it also came with great responsibility. The same tools that could build wonders could also cause destruction. The Atlanteans had understood this balance, using their knowledge to create structures that honoured the Earth and its gifts.

Elena reflected on the challenges facing modern civilization. The Atlanteans' mastery of metallurgy was a reminder of the importance of sustainability and respect for the natural world. Their ability to create without destroying was a lesson that humanity could not afford to ignore.

The fifth law, their mastery of metallurgy was a testament to their ingenuity, their skill, and their respect for the natural world. It was a legacy of craft and creativity; a reminder of what humanity could achieve when it worked in harmony with its environment.

Elena imagined the potential applications of this knowledge in the modern world. Advanced alloys could revolutionize construction, transportation, and energy, creating materials that were stronger, lighter, and more sustainable. The Atlanteans' approach to metallurgy—combining science, art, and respect for nature—offered a blueprint for a better future.

The 6th Law of Advancement – The Mastery of Water

The sixth law of advancement was a testament to the Atlanteans' understanding of one of the most vital and abundant resources on Earth: water. Carved into the ancient stone tablet, this law chronicled their deep respect for water as a life-giving force and their ingenuity in harnessing it to enhance and sustain their civilization. For the Atlanteans, water was not just a necessity; it was a source of power, a means of transport, and a vital element in their pursuit of progress.

As Elena traced the words on the tablet, she felt the sacred wisdom of the ancients wash over her like a gentle stream:

"Water, the lifeblood of our world, is abundant and essential. The more we master its use; the more life thrives. We built canals, creating pathways for ships to transport goods and people. We constructed great aqueducts, bringing water to the heart of our cities and towns, sustaining life and growth. Beyond this, we unlocked the power of hydrogen within water, using it to fuel our machines and drive progress. Water is a gift, a force of life and power. Use it wisely, for it holds the key to the future."

The sixth law began with a recognition of water's role as the lifeblood of the planet. The Atlanteans had understood that water was more than a resource—it was the foundation of all life. Every living being depended on it, and every civilization was shaped by its availability and use.

Elena reflected on how water had always been central to human progress. Rivers had given rise to the earliest civilizations, providing a source of sustenance, transportation, and fertile land. But the Atlanteans had taken this relationship with water to a new level, mastering its use in ways that elevated their society and set them apart from others.

One of the first applications of water mastery described in the inscription was the construction of canals. The Atlanteans had recognized the potential of water as a means of transportation, creating networks of canals that connected cities, towns, and regions. These man-made waterways allowed ships to move goods and people efficiently, fostering trade and cultural exchange.

Elena imagined the Atlantean canals, their waters alive with activity as ships glided along, carrying everything from food and raw materials to finished goods and travellers. These canals were not just functional—they were works of art, lined with polished stone and adorned with intricate carvings that celebrated the beauty and importance of water.

The canals had transformed the Atlantean world, turning vast distances into navigable pathways and linking communities in ways that strengthened their civilization.

The inscription also described the construction of aqueducts, another marvel of Atlantean engineering. These structures were designed to bring water from distant sources to the heart of cities and towns, ensuring a steady and reliable supply for drinking, agriculture, and sanitation.

Elena marvelled at the ingenuity of the Atlanteans, who had built aqueducts that spanned miles, crossing valleys and mountains with precision and grace. These towering structures were feats of engineering, combining form and function in a way that symbolized the Atlanteans' respect for water and their ability to harness it.

Aqueducts had been essential to the growth of Atlantean cities, providing the water needed to sustain large populations and enabling the development of advanced urban centres. They were a reminder of the Atlanteans' commitment to using their knowledge and skills to improve the lives of their people.

Their mastery of water—not only as a life-sustaining resource but also as a source of power that could fuel their machines and drive their progress. The Atlanteans had gone beyond using water for transport and irrigation; they had unlocked the hidden energy within water itself, harnessing hydrogen, one of its primary components, to power their civilization.

As Elena read the inscription, she marvelled at the ingenuity of the ancients:

"Water, the lifeblood of our world, is abundant and vital. Its power is hidden within. We learned to split water into hydrogen and oxygen, unlocking a boundless source of energy. Hydrogen, combined with oxygen and ignited by spark, fuels our machines, propels our ships, and powers our progress. This is the energy of the future, clean and eternal. Use it wisely, for it is a gift as great as the water itself."

The Atlanteans' mastery of water went far beyond canals, aqueducts, and irrigation. They had discovered how to separate water into its basic elements—hydrogen and oxygen—using a process that modern science would later call "electrolysis." By passing an electric current through water, they had been able to split it into hydrogen gas and oxygen gas, each of which could be harnessed for various purposes.

Hydrogen had become the cornerstone of their energy technology. The Atlanteans had recognized its potential as a clean and powerful fuel, one that could be used without depleting the Earth's resources or polluting its environment.

The inscription hinted at a groundbreaking innovation: the Atlanteans' use of hydrogen-powered machines. Elena's mind raced as she tried to piece together how this ancient civilization might have achieved such a feat. Drawing on modern knowledge, she imagined the Atlanteans developing a primitive internal combustion engine, similar in concept to the one created millennia later in 1807 by François Isaac de Rivaz.

The Atlanteans' hydrogen engine would have worked by combining hydrogen gas with oxygen in a controlled environment. When ignited by an electric spark, the mixture would combust, producing a powerful force that could drive pistons or turbines. This process would generate energy to power machines, from vehicles and ships to industrial equipment.

The beauty of this technology lay in its simplicity and efficiency. The only byproduct of hydrogen combustion was water vapor, making it a clean and sustainable energy source. For the Atlanteans, this innovation would have been nothing short of revolutionary, enabling them to power their civilization without relying on finite resources like coal or oil.

The inscription described hydrogen-powered machines being used in various aspects of Atlantean life. These machines were not only practical but also symbolic of the Atlanteans' ingenuity and their ability to harness the forces of nature.

Hydrogen engines powered ships and vehicles, allowing the Atlanteans to travel great distances efficiently. Their ships, equipped with hydrogen-fuelled engines, glided across the seas, connecting distant lands and fostering trade and cultural exchange. On land, hydrogen-powered vehicles transported goods and people, making travel faster and more reliable.

In the industrial sector, hydrogen engines drove machinery that was used for mining, manufacturing, and construction. These machines enabled the Atlanteans to extract resources from the Earth, forge metals, and build their monumental structures. The precision and power provided by hydrogen technology were essential to their mastery of metallurgy and stonework.

Hydrogen was also used as a source of energy to power homes, cities, and public works. The Atlanteans had developed systems for storing and distributing hydrogen, ensuring a steady supply of clean energy for their civilization. This technology had allowed them to create a sustainable and efficient energy grid, one that was both innovative and environmentally friendly.

A key component of the Atlanteans' hydrogen technology was the use of electric sparks to ignite the hydrogen-oxygen mixture. The inscription hinted at their understanding of electricity, another natural force that they had mastered.

Elena imagined the Atlanteans using devices similar to spark plugs, generating an electric spark to ignite the hydrogen fuel. These devices would have been simple yet highly effective, enabling the Atlanteans to harness the power of hydrogen with precision and control. The combination of electricity and hydrogen was a testament to their ability to integrate different technologies, creating systems that were greater than the sum of their parts.

The sixth law reflected the Atlanteans' commitment to sustainability and their respect for the natural world. By using hydrogen as a fuel, they had created a clean energy system that did not deplete the Earth's resources or harm its ecosystems. This approach stood in stark contrast to the modern world's reliance on fossil fuels, which had led to pollution, climate change, and environmental degradation.

The Atlanteans had understood that true progress required harmony with nature. Their hydrogen-powered machines were not just technological marvels—they were symbols of a civilization that had learned to live in balance with its environment.

As Elena studied the sixth law, she felt a deep sense of admiration for the Atlanteans. Their mastery of water and hydrogen was a reminder of humanity's potential to create a sustainable and prosperous future.

In the modern world, hydrogen power was beginning to gain attention as a clean energy solution, but it remained underdeveloped and underutilized. The Atlanteans' example offered valuable lessons, showing how hydrogen could be used to power machines, industries, and entire civilizations without causing harm to the planet.

Elena imagined a future where hydrogen-powered vehicles replaced gasoline engines, where hydrogen fuel cells provided clean energy for homes and cities, and where the world's reliance on fossil fuels became a thing of the past. The knowledge preserved in the sixth law could be the key to unlocking that future.

The sixth law was more than a record of Atlantean achievements—Water, with its hidden power of hydrogen, was a gift of the Earth, a resource that held the potential to transform the world. But with that gift came a responsibility to use it wisely and sustainably.

The Atlanteans had shown what was possible when humanity worked in harmony with nature, using its gifts to create a better world. The sixth law was a reminder that the answers to humanity's greatest challenges were often found in the natural world, waiting to be discovered and understood.

Water, the lifeblood of the planet, held the key to the future. And the wisdom of the Atlanteans offered a roadmap for unlocking its full potential. With hydrogen power, humanity could achieve progress that was not only sustainable but also transformative, creating a world where technology and nature worked hand in hand.

The 7th Law of Advancement- The Power of Thought

The seventh and final law of advancement was the most profound and mysterious of all. It delved into the very essence of human existence, creativity, and connection. Unlike the other laws, which focused on the mastery of external forces—water, metallurgy, and electromagnetism—this law turned inward, exploring the boundless potential of the human mind. To the Atlanteans, thought was the ultimate power, the seed from which all creation sprang, and the force that connected every individual to the collective consciousness of humanity.

As Elena read the inscription, she felt a sense of awe and wonder:

"Thought is the source of all creation. Before anything is built, before anything is discovered, before any action is taken, there is thought. Thought gave rise to civilization and connects us to all who came before us. Through our DNA, we are linked to our ancestors, their thoughts and knowledge flowing through us. The power of thought is limitless. Through meditation, one can tune the mind to the universal stream of thought, where every idea ever conceived still exists as electrical waves. Intuition is the ability to receive these thoughts, a connection to the collective knowledge of all who have lived. This stream of thought, enriched by civilizations more advanced than our own, is waiting to be tapped. Master the power of thought, and there is no limit to what you can achieve."

The inscription began with a truth so simple yet so profound: everything created by humanity began as a single thought. Every invention, every piece of art, every structure, and every advancement was born in the mind of a thinker. Thought was the origin of creation, the spark that set the wheels of progress in motion.

The Atlanteans understood that thought was not just a tool but a force of nature, one that could shape the world as powerfully as fire, water, or stone. Their reverence for thought reflected their belief in the boundless potential of the human mind. To them, thought was the ultimate resource, the wellspring of all innovation and discovery.

Elena reflected on this idea, realizing how much of modern civilization owed to the power of thought. Everything—from the wheel to the internet—had started as a spark of inspiration in the mind of a single individual. The Atlanteans' recognition of this truth was a reminder of the incredible potential within every human being.

The seventh law also emphasized the deep connection between individuals and their ancestors. The Atlanteans had understood that DNA was not just a physical blueprint but also a link to the past. Through their DNA, individuals carried the legacy of their predecessors, their thoughts, experiences, and knowledge encoded within them.

This idea resonated deeply with Elena. She imagined the Atlanteans viewing themselves not as isolated beings but as part of an unbroken chain of humanity, stretching back through time. Their ancestors' thoughts and ideas were not lost—they were preserved within them, waiting to be awakened.

The inscription suggested that this connection was not merely symbolic but real. Through meditation and the power of thought, the Atlanteans had learned to access the collective knowledge of their ancestors, tapping into a vast reservoir of wisdom and experience.

At the heart of the seventh law was the concept of a universal stream of thought—a continuous flow of ideas, knowledge, and intuition that existed beyond the confines of time and space. The Atlanteans believed that every thought ever conceived still existed as electrical waves or thought waves, permeating the universe.

Through meditation, they had discovered how to tune their minds to this stream, becoming receivers for the thoughts and ideas of others. Elena was fascinated by this idea, likening it to a radio picking up signals on the same frequency. Intuition, according to the Atlanteans, was not a random occurrence but a direct connection to this universal stream. When someone had a sudden insight or a "gut feeling," they were tuning into thoughts that resonated with their own wavelength.

This explained why some individuals seemed to possess extraordinary creativity or foresight—they had learned, consciously or unconsciously, to tap into the stream of thought. For the Atlanteans, this ability was not a rare gift but a skill that could be cultivated through meditation and mental discipline.

One of the most remarkable aspects of the seventh law was its assertion that the universal stream of thought contained the ideas of civilizations more advanced than the current one. The Atlanteans believed that humanity was not progressing in a straight line but was part of a cyclical process, with periods of great advancement followed by decline.

Elena was struck by the implication: the knowledge and ideas of these advanced civilizations were not lost but preserved in the stream of thought, waiting to be rediscovered. The Atlanteans themselves had drawn on this legacy, using it to achieve their remarkable advancements in science, engineering, and philosophy.

This realization filled Elena with a sense of possibility. The answers to humanity's greatest challenges—clean energy, sustainable living, and even the mysteries of the universe—might already exist, waiting to be tapped into by those who could access the universal stream of thought.

The inscription emphasized the importance of meditation as the key to unlocking the power of thought. The Atlanteans had developed techniques for quieting the mind, focusing their thoughts, and tuning into the universal stream. Through meditation, they had trained their minds to become receivers, capable of picking up thoughts and ideas from the collective consciousness.

Elena imagined the Atlanteans sitting in serene meditation, their minds open and attuned to the flow of thought. This practice had not only enhanced their creativity and intuition but also deepened their connection to one another and to the universe.

Meditation, as described by the seventh law, was not just a spiritual practice—it was a tool for innovation, discovery, and progress. By mastering their thoughts, the Atlanteans had unlocked a power greater than any physical resource: the limitless potential of the human mind.

The seventh law concluded with a profound truth: there was no limit to the power of thought. The human mind, when properly trained and focused, was capable of achieving anything. The Atlanteans had understood this, using the power of thought to shape their civilization and create a legacy that endured long after their physical world had vanished.

Elena felt a deep sense of inspiration as she contemplated the seventh law. It was a reminder that the greatest resource was not in the

Earth, the seas, or the skies—it was within. The power of thought, the ability to imagine, create, and connect, was the true force that drove progress and defined humanity.

As Elena studied the seventh law, she felt a renewed sense of purpose. The Atlanteans had left behind a message of hope and possibility, a reminder that humanity's greatest achievements began as a single thought.

The seventh law was a challenge to tap into the universal stream of thought and unlock the limitless potential of the mind. It was a reminder that the answers to humanity's greatest challenges were already within reach, waiting to be discovered by those who dared to think, dream, and create.

Elena felt a profound connection to the Atlanteans and to the countless generations of thinkers, dreamers, and creators who had come before her. The journey through the laws of advancement was complete, but her own journey was just beginning.

The power of thought, the greatest force in the universe, was hers to wield. And with it, there was no limit to what she could achieve.

The weight of these discoveries pressed upon her, a blend of triumph and longing. How she wished her father could stand beside her, sharing in the moment they had both worked so tirelessly to reach. Yet, even in his absence, Elena felt his presence keenly, as if his spirit and that of Thothamak were woven into the fabric of the chamber, urging her forward.

The realization that she held in her hands the culmination of centuries of exploration and speculation was overwhelming. These tablets were more than just relics; they were a roadmap for humanity's potential, a testament to the power of knowledge and the promise of a brighter future. The advanced technology and wisdom of Atlantis, long considered myth, were now within her grasp.

Elena knew that the significance of this moment extended far beyond personal achievement. The teachings contained within these tablets could serve as a catalyst for a new era of enlightenment, guiding humanity back onto a path of unity, innovation, and peace. It was a responsibility she could not take lightly, nor was it one she could shoulder alone.

Her father had always believed in the transformative power of knowledge, and Elena was determined to honour that belief by sharing these discoveries with the world. It was time to bring the wisdom of Atlantis out of the shadows and into the light, to ignite a renaissance of understanding and possibility.

With reverence and care, Elena began the painstaking process of documenting her findings, ensuring that the integrity of each piece was preserved. She understood the importance of sharing this knowledge responsibly, aware of its potential to reshape the course of history.

As she worked, she felt a sense of clarity and purpose enveloping her. The journey that had begun with Thothamak, and had been continued by her father, was now hers to lead. She would be the bridge between ancient wisdom and modern understanding, a steward of the

Atlantean legacy charged with guiding humanity toward its highest potential.

She knew when first revealed these would be greeted with both scepticism and wonder. But she was ready to face it, empowered by the knowledge that she was part of something far greater than herself. The legacy of Atlantis, preserved through the ages, would serve as a beacon of hope and enlightenment for all who dared to dream of a better world.

With the tablets secured and her resolve strengthened, Elena prepared to emerge from the Labyrinth. The discoveries she carried would soon be revealed to the world, a testament to the enduring spirit of exploration and the unyielding quest for truth. Humanity was on the brink of a new dawn, and Elena was determined to light the way.

Elena Finding Her Father's Journals

Epilogue: The Next Wave

The room was silent except for the low hum of computers and the occasional click of a keyboard. The observatory, nestled high in the mountains, was a sanctuary of science, its walls lined with monitors, charts, and telescopes that peered deep into the cosmos. It was a clear night, the kind that astronomers loved, with the stars scattered like glitter across the velvet black sky.

Dr. Marcus Caldwell, the lead astrophysicist, leaned forward in his chair, his eyes fixed on the screen in front of him. His brow furrowed as he studied the data streaming in from the observatory's most powerful telescope. Beside him, a young intern, Sophie Chen, shifted nervously, her fingers drumming on the desk.

"Are you seeing this?" Marcus murmured, his voice barely above a whisper.

Sophie nodded; her eyes wide. "It's definitely not a glitch. The trajectory... it's consistent."

Marcus exhaled slowly, the weight of the realization settling over him. He tapped a few keys, bringing up the calculations they had run moments earlier. The numbers didn't lie. Far out in the solar system, beyond the orbit of Jupiter, a comet had been detected. Its icy core glinted faintly in the light of a distant sun as it hurtled through the void, a cosmic traveller on a collision course with Earth.

The comet was roughly two miles across, a monstrous chunk of ice, rock, and dust. Its long, elliptical orbit suggested it had been lurking in the outer reaches of the solar system for eons, undisturbed and unnoticed. But something—perhaps the gravitational pull of a passing planet or the subtle nudge of a celestial body—had altered its path, sending it hurtling toward the inner solar system.

Marcus ran the calculations again, his fingers trembling slightly on the keyboard. The projected impact date was just over a year away. A year. Twelve months. Three hundred and sixty-five days. That was all the time humanity had to prepare.

He turned to Sophie, his voice steady but urgent. "Send this to the International Planetary Defence Coalition. They need to see this immediately. Flag it as priority one."

Sophie hesitated for only a moment before nodding and typing furiously, her hands shaking as she composed the message. This was no ordinary find. Comets were fascinating, yes, but this one was different. This one was dangerous.

As the data pinged across the globe to observatories and space agencies, Marcus stood and paced the room, his mind racing. A two-mile-wide comet was catastrophic. It wasn't large enough to wipe out all life on Earth—that was the territory of six-mile asteroids like the one that had doomed the dinosaurs—but it was more than enough to cause widespread devastation.

If it impacted land, the explosion would be beyond comprehension, levelling cities, creating massive firestorms, and throwing debris high into the atmosphere, blocking sunlight and disrupting the climate. If it struck the ocean, the resulting tsunamis would be hundreds of feet high, swallowing entire coastlines and causing untold destruction.

Either way, the loss of life would be unimaginable. Civilization as they knew it would hang in the balance.

But Marcus also knew that humanity had come a long way since the days of the dinosaurs. The seventh law of advancement—the power of thought—flashed in his mind like a beacon of hope. They had tools, technology, and knowledge that ancient civilizations could have only dreamed of. They had the ability to detect threats like this and, perhaps, even the ability to stop them.

By the next morning, news of the comet had spread like wildfire through the scientific community. Meetings were convened, task forces assembled, and plans drafted. The world's leading experts in astronomy, engineering, and planetary defence were brought together in a race against time.

At the forefront of the effort was the International Planetary Défense Coalition (IPDC), a global organization formed after near-misses with asteroids in the previous decades. Their mission was clear: to develop a plan to deflect or destroy the comet before it could reach Earth.

Ideas flooded in—nuclear detonations to alter the comet's course, kinetic impactors to nudge it off trajectory, even ambitious schemes to use solar sails or gravitational tractors to steer it away. Each concept was scrutinized, debated, and tested in simulations.

But time was short, and the challenges were immense. The comet was still far away, moving at a staggering speed, and any mission to intercept it would require pinpoint precision and flawless execution.

As the days turned into weeks, something extraordinary began to happen. The looming threat of the comet brought humanity together in a way that few events ever had. Political rivalries and national borders faded into the background as countries pooled their resources and expertise.

Scientists worked side by side, sharing data and ideas. Engineers collaborated across continents, designing spacecraft and propulsion systems. The public, too, rallied behind the effort, their fears tempered by a shared determination to face the challenge head-on.

For the first time in decades, it felt as though the world was united—not in fear, but in hope.

As Marcus watched the efforts unfold, he couldn't help but think of the seventh law of advancement. The power of thought, the ability to tap into the collective knowledge and creativity of humanity, was the driving force behind everything they were doing.

Every idea, every innovation, every solution had started as a thought—a spark in the mind of an individual that had grown into something greater. The scientists and engineers working to save the planet were drawing not only on their own knowledge but also on the accumulated wisdom of their ancestors, the breakthroughs of past generations, and the intuition that came from tuning into the universal stream of thought.

The Atlanteans had understood this power, and now, in the face of an existential threat, humanity was rediscovering it.

As the weeks turned into months, the mission to intercept the comet took shape. A fleet of spacecraft, equipped with cutting-edge technology, was launched into the void, carrying humanity's hopes and dreams with them.

The outcome of the mission was uncertain, but one thing was clear: the comet had reminded humanity of its greatest strength—the power to think, to create, and to come together in the face of adversity.

For Marcus, Sophie, and the countless others who had worked tirelessly to prepare for the challenge, the comet was not just a threat—it was an opportunity. An opportunity to prove that the power of thought, the greatest law of advancement, was limitless.

As the observatory's telescope tracked the spacecraft speeding toward the comet, Marcus felt a sense of awe and determination. The future was uncertain, but humanity was ready to face it, armed with the greatest tool of all: the power of thought.

And perhaps, just perhaps, they were not alone. Somewhere in the universal stream of thought, the wisdom of the ancients was with them, guiding their way.

The battle for Earth's survival had begun. And with it, the dawn of a new era.

A New Threat Enters Our Cosmos

About The Author

Richard Eckley is a multifaceted author, educator, and thought leader who bridges the gap between ancient wisdom and modern understanding. As the founder of the Eckley Global Community School, he has dedicated his life to expanding minds and challenging conventional thinking.

His bestselling "Coffee Reads" series has helped thousands of readers transform their lives through practical approaches to health, wealth, relationships, and mindset development. Known for his ability to distill complex concepts into accessible wisdom, Eckley brings this same clarity to his exploration of ancient mysteries.

Eckley's fascination with historical enigmas began in the 1980s while watching Arthur C. Clarke's Mysterious World, but it was a birthday gift from his wife - "Queen Moo and the Egyptian Sphinx" - that reignited his passion and set him on a path of intensive research. This journey led him to question established theories about ancient transatlantic connections and pre-flood civilizations.

In "Atlantis: A New Theory," Eckley combines decades of research with hands-on investigation, including expeditions to the Azores archipelago. His work delves deep into Plato's original texts while drawing connections between global flood myths and archaeological evidence of advanced ancient civilizations. Through meticulous analysis of historical records, geological data, and archaeological findings, Eckley presents a compelling new perspective on the location and nature of Atlantis.

As a podcaster and educator, Eckley continues to challenge historical paradigms while making ancient mysteries accessible to modern audiences. His work demonstrates that the past is not just a collection of stories, but a living source of wisdom that can reshape our understanding of human civilization.

you can get in touch with him at...

https://eckleyglobalcommunityschool.com/

email   egcs24@yahoo.com

linkedin.com/in/richard-eckley-41966936

https://www.facebook.com/rickeckley67/

Also by

"Atlantis: A New Theory"
Richard Eckley presents an intriguing new perspective on one of history's most enduring mysteries in his thought-provoking work "Atlantis: A New Theory." By combining ancient texts, particularly Plato's detailed accounts, with modern scientific discoveries and geological evidence, Eckley constructs a compelling argument for both the existence and location of the legendary civilization.

The book's strength lies in how it addresses the three main objections scholars have traditionally raised about Atlantis: its supposed age (9,000 years before Plato), its sudden disappearance in a day and night, and its location beyond the Pillars of Hercules. Eckley tackles these challenges by connecting recent archaeological discoveries, like Göbekli Tepe, with evidence of ancient impact events, particularly the Hiawatha crater in Greenland.

Most notably, Eckley proposes that Atlantis was located along the Mid-Atlantic Ridge, with parts of it now forming the Azores archipelago. He presents evidence including ancient cart tracks, pyramidal structures, and underwater formations that suggest human habitation predating Portuguese settlement. His theory about how a massive asteroid impact in Greenland could have triggered a cascade of catastrophic events - including mega-tsunamis, volcanic eruptions, and sudden sea-level rises - offers a plausible explanation for Atlantis's rapid demise.

The author's writing style is accessible, combining scholarly analysis with engaging narrative. He effectively uses modern analogies, like the 2011 Japanese tsunami, to help readers understand the scale of ancient catastrophes. The inclusion of numerous photographs, diagrams, and maps helps visualize his arguments.

While some may find certain theories speculative, Eckley's work contributes meaningfully to the ongoing discussion about prehistoric civilizations and their potential technological achievements. The book challenges conventional timelines of human civilization while remaining grounded in geological and archaeological evidence.

"Atlantis: A New Theory" will appeal to both serious researchers of ancient civilizations and general readers interested in alternative historical perspectives. It offers a fresh examination of an age-old mystery while raising important questions about our understanding of human prehistory.

Your 4 Keys to A Healthier Happier You
What an amazing read this book really is. I first came across Richard on Linkedin and he made me an offer on his book I simply could

not resist. At first, I did not know what to expect, but boy am I glad I made that decision to buy the book and have a read. First of all, what a minefield of information and some reminders of how we find that happier healthier you. The book is an easy quick read and is just filled with brilliant reminders of daily life choices that we are free to make. It explains why we feel like we do, and also explains why others behave and feel they way they do too. The book is written in such an informative way and does not fill you with dread of not knowing what those fancy words mean. This is a book that I will read time after time and have no hesitation in recommending to others. Gwenn Baird

MASTERING YOUR MINDSET

Richard Eckley's "Mastering your Mindset" takes you on a journey going back more than a billion years to help understand how we have evolved into the human race we are today. The science behind our evolution is described succinctly in layman's terms with snippets of history along the way. The book clearly demonstrates how this development has gained velocity drastically over the more recent years of our planet's existence, linking this to our changing anatomy and brain development. Richard empowers the reader to realise that they can change and create their beliefs rather than going to the grave carrying those passed onto us from previous generations. He challenges you to question the origin of beliefs, explaining that choosing to change them can completely alter the direction of your life. This leads into how to master our mindset, using analogies and short stories to explain how to set the wheels in motion to stretch ourselves beyond our comfort zone to a better more fulfilling life. The importance of repetition and feeding our subconscious with positivity through personal development books and audios is discussed. Richard then explains all the development in our world has come from someone's initial vision and their belief in themselves, to pursue it even with all its failures during the process. The reader is then encouraged to consider their own vision for the next five years with a series of suggestions around things such as health, wealth and relationships. As the book draws to a close, the importance of an experienced mentor and setting goals is discussed, repeating the importance of repetition in the pursuit of achieving the goals you have set for yourself. The book is an extremely interesting and thought provoking read, explaining mindset in easy-to-understand terms, leaving those truly interested, wanting to know more. Richard's forthcoming books in the "Mastering Your Mindset" series will surely be well received by his readers. —Stuart James Dickson

HOW TO MASTER YOUR HEALTH

Richard Eckley's book 'How To Master your Health' is well worth a read and if you haven't come across his books before then this is a great one to start your journey. The information and guidance in this book is presented in a very readable and easy to follow manner and each chapter ends with a summary of the key points in it; in fact these will help you develop a personal checklist on how to 'master' your health. Richard starts with an introduction which sets out the evolution of our eating habits that underpin our current problems with diet and lifestyle related health issues. Each chapter builds on how we can improve and/or regain a better quality of life with regard to our personal health through changes to eating, drinking, sleeping and breathing. Chapter by chapter he shows us how wecan improve our health through making relatively simple decisions/choices and taking personal control through achievable actions. The key health areas he focuses on are those that are of most prevalence in the western world today- Alzheimer's, heart disease and strokes, cancer and the impact of obesity. Richard looks at all of these health issues which undoubtedly are clogging up our NHS and its ability to treat us. He gives us a proactive way to take back control of our own health and promote a longer life well lived. This philosophy is one we all need to consider about how we can achieve a long and healthy life through making better personal choices on our diet, exercise, breathing and sleeping patterns, rather than focusing on treating with drugs individual symptoms that in the main are caused by not looking after ourselves. I for one will be reviewing my lifestyle choices and taking on board the easy steps I can take to make my life healthier and I'll remember Richard's words 'life is a journey and not a destination', I want to enjoy my trip to the fullest!! —Sharon Pruski (food Scientist & home economics teacher)

HOW TO CREATE WEALTH

The first chapters of the book delve into the origins of money, providing readers with a fascinating historical context for understanding its role in society. By tracing the evolution of currency and its impact on human civilization, the author sets the stage for a deeper comprehension of wealth and its creation. One of the book's strengths lies in its clear and straightforward writing style. The author avoids unnecessary jargon and presents complex financial concepts in a manner that is easily understandable to both novices and seasoned investors. This approach makes the book accessible to a wide range of readers, regardless of their prior knowledge of finance. The inclusion of backstories of renowned millionaires and billionaires, such as Richard Branson, Jeff Bezos, Sara Blakely, J.K. Rowling, Arnold Schwarzenegger and many more, adds a human touch to the book. These captivating success stories not only inspire readers but also offer valuable lessons in determination, resilience, and entrepreneurial spirit. By examining the journeys of these iconic individuals, the book highlights the diverse paths to wealth and underscores the importance of passion and perseverance. Additionally, the author's insightful analysis of successful companies like Rolls-Royce, Cadbury Chocolate, Coca-Cloa, Costa Coffee plus others giving their origin stories provides readers with realworld examples of effective wealth-building strategies. By studying the business practices and strategies of these enterprises, readers can gain valuable insights into the principles that drive sustainable wealth creation on an organizational level. The core of the book is its 10-step path to creating wealth, which offers a practical and actionable roadmap for readers to follow. Each step is well-explained, making it easier for readers to apply the concepts to their own financial endeavours. The book covers crucial aspects such as setting financial goals, managing investments, building multiple income streams, and cultivating a positive money mindset. Throughout the book, the writing style remains engaging and accessible. Complex financial concepts are broken down into easily digestible portions, making it suitable for readers with varying levels of financial literacy. The combination of historical insights, real-life success stories, and practical advice creates a well-rounded and enriching reading experience. One of the few potential drawbacks of the book is its brevity. Some readers might wish for more in-depth exploration of certain topics or real-life case studies to illustrate the principles in action. However, it is important to note that the book's concise nature is intentional, aiming to provide readers with a quick and practical reference guide. In conclusion, "How to

Create Wealth" is a must-read for anyone seeking to understand the intricacies of wealth creation. Its well-researched historical insights, inspiring stories of successful individuals and companies, and the practical 10-step path make it a comprehensive and empowering resource. Whether you are a budding entrepreneur, an aspiring investor, or simply someone looking to improve their financial situation, this book provides valuable guidance to help you embark on your journey to financial prosperity.

HOW TO DEVELOP BETTER RELATIONSHIPS

"How to Develop Better Relationships" guides readers through the lifecycle of relationships, offering practical advice and deep reflections tailored to enhance any partnership. The book is organized into ten critical stages, each addressing a different aspect of relationships, making it a comprehensive guide for anyone looking to deepen their understanding of relationship dynamics. The journey begins with "Where It All Began," exploring how early observations and interactions shape our expectations and behaviours in relationships. "Your Experiences Growing Up" continues to build on this foundation, examining the influence of childhood and adolescence on our romantic connections. "Looking for Love" shifts focus to the search for a romantic partner, discussing common pitfalls and strategies for finding someone who complements and supports your life goals and values. "The Honeymoon Period" describes the early blissful phase of relationships, offering tips on enjoying this time while laying the groundwork for a deeper connection. "Adjusting to Living Together" provides a practical guide to one of the biggest transitions for couples, offering strategies for dealing with common challenges that come with sharing a space. "Family Life" addresses the changes couples face when relationships evolve to include children, emphasizing the importance of maintaining a strong partnership amidst the demands of parenting. "The Empty Nest Syndrome" tackles the emotional and relationship shifts that occur when children grow up and move out, providing guidance on how to rediscover and reinvent the partnership during this phase. "His Cave/Her Friends" discusses the balance of independence and togetherness in maintaining a healthy relationship, recognizing the need for personal space and social outlets outside the relationship. "Midlife Crisis/Erectile Dysfunction and Menopause" addresses the physical and psychological challenges couples may face in middle age, offering compassionate advice for navigating these sensitive issues together. The book concludes with "The Ultimate Balance," synthesizing all insights from the previous chapters into a cohesive guide on achieving balance, fulfilment, and enduring love in relationships. "How to Develop Better Relationships" is not just a book but a resource that couples can return to at each stage of their journey together. Its blend of practical advice, psychological insights, and empathetic tone makes it an essential guide for anyone committed to building and sustaining a loving, healthy relationship.

CREATE THE LIFE YOU WANT

At Eckley Global Community School we empower our students to become the best version of themselves, using the unique Eckley S.I.T.T. system

WE ARE AN ONLINE SCHOOL TEACHING THE 4 KEYS TO SUCCESS

HEALTH, WEALTH, RELATIONSHIP & MINDSET

Teaching the Entrepreneurs of tomorrow how to find their passion today.

We are your college in your pocket

On completion of all homework to the required standards students will receive their diploma 30 days later.

CONTACT US

egcs24@yahoo.com

and get a free digital copy of

www.ingramcontent.com/pod-product-compliance
Lightning Source LLC
Chambersburg PA
CBHW051605010526
44119CB00056B/787